Developing
INSTRUCTIONAL LEADERSHIP

Developing
INSTRUCTIONAL
LEADERSHIP

Creating a Culture of
Ownership through the Use of
Strategic Learning Practices

ROBERT CROWE AND JANE KENNEDY

1641 Worthington Road, Ste. 210
West Palm Beach, FL 33409
724.459.2100
Email: learningsciences.com
learningsciences.com

Library of Congress Control Number: 2020950641

22 21 20 19 18   1 2 3 4 5

Publisher's Cataloging-in-Publication Data
provided by Five Rainbows Cataloging Services

Names: Crowe, Robert, author. | Kennedy, Jane, author.
Title: Developing instructional leadership : creating a culture of ownership through the use of strategic learning practices / Robert Crowe [and] Jane Kennedy.
Description: West Palm Beach, FL : Learning Sciences, 2020.
Identifiers: LCCN 2020950641 (print) | ISBN 978-1-943920-78-5 (paperback) | ISBN 978-1-941112-23-6 (ebook)
Subjects: LCSH: School principals. | Educational leadership. | School management and organization. | Education—Aims and objectives. | Academic achievement. | BISAC: EDUCATION / Administration / School Superintendents & Principals. | EDUCATION / Leadership. | EDUCATION / Administration / Elementary & Secondary. | EDUCATION / Aims & Objectives.
Classification: LCC LB2831.9 .C76 2020 (print) | LCC LB2831.9 (ebook) | DDC 371.2—dc23.

TABLE OF CONTENTS

2 Instruction 43
The Value of Adult Learning Strategies

3 Assessment 69
The Value of Monitoring Learning Strategies

4 Climate **95**

The Value of a Professional Learning Environment

5 Instructional Leadership in Action **121**

A Vignette About Implementing
a Hybrid Learning Model

6 Differentiated Delegation **135**

How to Ensure Individual Success

FOREWORD

If you have opened this book and are reading this page, you are likely a person who understands that effective classroom instruction serves as the foundation for increased student learning for all students. You likely also have some understanding of the important role school administrators play in providing instructional leadership to support and improve classroom teaching.

You may be an educator who is already serving as an instructional leader in a school, an instructional coach who provides support and guidance to classroom teachers, or a district administrator who is looking to improve the instructional leadership capacity of those you lead. No matter who you are or what your current position, you've picked up the right book. It is one I wish I had as an aspiring school and district leader when I began my instructional leadership work 25 years ago.

As a new classroom teacher in 1990, I was fortunate to begin my career in a school district with a strong and always improving instructional culture. I was part of a school where we, as classroom teachers, were expected to design lessons based on content standards with clear learning objectives; ones that aligned learning activities and processes to those objectives and provided for meaningful opportunities for engagement of all learners.

Knowing how to do this well was not left to chance. The instructional leaders in my district were highly supported and trained in how to provide the leadership necessary to improve classroom instruction to raise student achievement. I was fortunate to work alongside one of these leaders as a teacher, and she served as my first model of effective instructional leadership and inspired me to become that kind of leader myself.

I went on to become a site administrator for over a decade with the goal of providing the instructional leadership and support necessary for classroom teachers to bring about higher achievement for all students. In four different schools, it was the joy of my life to work alongside teachers who cared deeply about their practice and who were committed to improving every day to enhance learning for their students.

Those experiences still directly influence the work I do today. They helped me deeply understand that high quality instruction every day for all students, in an environment that honors and nurtures their unique gifts and interests, is the lynchpin for their future success.

My years as a school principal were the best of my career—that is until I became a school superintendent! Creating the conditions in which the people I lead can do their best work for students is my calling.

That's also the calling of the authors of this book.

I first met Bob (and later Jane) when I became a school superintendent over 10 years ago. I was inspired to bring the instructional leadership skills and experiences I had gained over the 20 years before to my work as a district superintendent, but the work of a school superintendent is not done alone. As Jon Gordon writes in his book, *The Power of a Positive Team*, "No one creates great things alone. We all need a team to be successful. We are better together, and together we can accomplish great things."

It takes a talented team of leaders, teachers, and support staff to bring a strong school and district instructional culture to life. It also takes the support from sage advisors and external partners. That is where Bob and Jane came in.

Bob joined our team in 2011 as a collaborative partner and consultant to support our efforts in developing the instructional leadership skills of our administrators and the instructional practices of our teachers. Since that time, Jane joined us in the work, and with their knowledge, insights, and experience in developing the actions of effective instructional leaders, we continue to grow and evolve in our work. This book reflects their knowledge, skills, and experience.

Instructional leadership skills can be learned, and this book offers a research-based framework of the actions school leaders must take to support, influence, and motivate teachers as they implement new initiatives to improve student learning. It provides a clear pathway for leaders to build the capacity and responsibility of teachers by taking clear and consistent actions every day in the areas of **curriculum, instruction, assessment,** and **climate** to increase opportunities for student learning. You will learn that if we, as leaders, take actionable steps in each of these areas, we can support teachers with the effective instructional leadership needed to improve student achievement.

Bob and Jane's extensive lived experiences working with countless leaders, teachers, and students from across the country, combined with the best research on what actually makes a difference in student learning and school leadership will contribute greatly to your work in becoming the best instructional leader you can be.

Dr. Candace Singh
Superintendent, Fallbrook Union Elementary School District
Founder, AASA Aspiring Superintendents Academy for Female Leaders
AASA Executive Committee Member (2017–2020)

ABOUT THE AUTHORS

Robert Crowe

Bob is one of the co-founders of Elevated Achievement Group, a professional learning company dedicated to helping educators develop student ownership at all grade levels and at all types of schools. His work led him to co-write the book *Developing Student Ownership,* which is a practical guide for educators to motivate students to own their own learning. Bob began his tenure in education as a bilingual teacher in Southern California in 1993, when he taught English learners at all proficiency levels. Since then, he has worked extensively across the United States supporting administrators, teachers, students, and parents at all school levels to implement standards-based curriculum, instruction, and assessment.

Jane Kennedy

Jane is co-author of the book *Developing Student Ownership* and is co-founder of Elevated Achievement Group. She founded this professional learning company with the express desire to focus on supporting educators as she feels they need to be supported—with a collaborative approach instead of a top-down approach. Jane began her career in 1991 on the east coast as a self-contained classroom teacher in a diverse school setting with a majority of her students receiving Title I support. This initial experience infused Jane with a passion for educational equity that has influenced her subsequent career focus. This focus led her to begin consulting work with a national textbook publisher where she supported adults at all levels in the educational system. She then used the skills she acquired to develop processes that support the implementation of research-based reforms that focus on increasing student ownership and developing instructional leadership.

ACKNOWLEDGMENTS

We would like to thank our friends and fellow educators for supporting our work in developing authentic student ownership and instructional leadership, specifically the outstanding students, teachers, and administrators at the following districts and schools:

- **ABC Unified School District:** Cerritos, California
- **ACT Academy Cyber Charter High School:** Philadelphia, Pennsylvania
- **Ad Prima Charter Schools:** Philadelphia, Pennsylvania
- **Austin Independent School District:** Austin, Texas
- **California State University, San Bernardino GEAR UP:** San Bernardino, California
- **Fallbrook Union Elementary School District:** Fallbrook, California
- **Fullerton Joint Union High School District:** Fullerton, California
- **Hacienda La Puente Unified School District:** City of Industry, California
- **Harambee Institute of Science & Technology Charter School:** Philadelphia, Pennsylvania
- **Komarek School District 94:** North Riverside, Illinois
- **Perris Union High School District:** Perris, California
- **Saddleback Valley Unified School District:** Mission Viejo, California
- **San Bernardino City Unified School District:** San Bernardino, California

- **Santa Maria Joint Union High School District:** Santa Maria, California
- **Sequoia Union High School District:** Redwood City, California
- **Walnut Valley Unified School District:** Walnut, California
- **Winslow Township School District:** Atco, New Jersey
- **Youngstown City School District:** Youngstown, Ohio

Remember, principals model the thinking behind the ownership and explicitly address the skills of ownership. This takes planning. In order for all stakeholders to successfully support an initiative focused on increasing student achievement, principals must be strategic in the actions they use to support staff.

—Robert Crowe and Jane Kennedy

INTRODUCTION
The Power of Instructional Leadership

Dear principal, before you begin reading our book, we're going to ask you to pause for a moment and think about your perfect school. This could be the school you had in mind when you decided to go into administration. This could be the school you've heard about but have never seen in action. This could be the dream school you are building right now.

At this school, what are the students saying and doing? What are the teachers saying and doing? What are you saying and doing?

We bet it probably looks and sounds something like this . . .

If we popped into a classroom, we'd hear students explaining what they were learning, why they are learning it, and what ultimate success looks like. We'd see students working in groups and helping their classmates understand the work. We'd read individual reflections about how they learn and what they do when they struggle. If we spoke with students, they'd be able to tell us how they will use their learning in the future. We'd see kids who love learning and are achieving higher and higher year by year.

If we dropped into a different classroom, we'd hear the teacher clearly articulating the skill that the students would be learning that day and what mastery looked like and when they could expect it to occur. We'd see teachers offering feedback to students, modeling how to support each other in groups and how to take academic risks. If we spoke with teachers, they'd be able to tell us the schoolwide initiative to increase achievement and their specific role in that. If we attended a meeting, we'd see them working with their colleagues to clarify their understanding of the initiative and we'd hear them ask the principal for help and support. We'd see teachers who own their role as the professional decision-maker whose job is to ensure student success.

And what are you doing in this perfect school?

If we visited the front office, we'd meet a principal who sees the teachers as individual learners. If we asked, we'd hear the principal explaining the long-term goal for increasing student achievement, the current initiative to support this goal, and the criteria of successful implementation. If we looked at the professional development calendar, we'd see the plan of support for the teachers, including learning opportunities and monitoring. If we sat in a classroom observation debrief, we'd hear the principal asking the teacher a series of questions to fully understand their decision-making. We'd see a principal that supported and respected the decision-making abilities of their teachers.

In this dream school, we'd be seeing and hearing an example of support for all stakeholders. We'd be seeing and hearing the actions of instructional leadership.

Now, back to reality. How close is your current school to your dream school? Is your dream a pipe dream? Do you believe that your dream can even exist?

We do.

We do because we know that you are the key to whatever school you want to lead. Now, we aren't saying this is something you can do overnight, but the research bears out that you have the power to turn your school into your dream school. According to Leithwood, Seashore Louis, Anderson, and Wahlstrom (2004) in their review of research on how leadership influences student learning,

> Leadership is second only to classroom instruction among all school-related factors that contribute to what students learn at school . . .

> While the evidence shows small but significant effects of leadership actions on student learning across the spectrum of schools, existing research also shows that demonstrated effects of successful leadership are considerably greater in schools that are

in more difficult circumstances. Indeed, there are virtually no documented instances of troubled schools being turned around without intervention by a powerful leader. Many other factors may contribute to such turnarounds, but leadership is the catalyst. (p. 5)

Of all the skills a principal needs to succeed, the most vital, in terms of increasing academic achievement, is that of instructional leadership. The skill of instructional leadership is made up of actions that can be seen and heard, and we believe that the actions of instructional leadership can be developed.

You believe this, too; otherwise you would not have picked up this book. It is designed as a manual to guide current principals, assistant principals, and future administrators as you turn your dream into your reality.

We want to support you in building your dream school. That's why in this book we will show you the actions you need to incorporate into your management style to develop effective and efficient instructional leadership.

The Actions of Instructional Leadership

What is leadership? If you were to look up this word, you would find myriad definitions. But, regardless of the intent or details of the wording, most definitions will identify leadership in some form or fashion as *the art of inspiring a group of people toward achieving a common goal.* This reminds us that regardless of the business being led, leadership is linked to a goal. It is no different in education. So, when we talk about leadership in the context of education, we know we are talking about the art of inspiring a group of people toward achieving a common set of goals for learning and academic achievement.

However, we are less concerned with a definition and more concerned with the practical answer to the question "What are the actions of a principal who effectively leads a school with the performance outcome of increased academic achievement for each and every student?"

In other words, "What are the actions of instructional leadership?" For us, the actions of instructional leadership fall into a framework with four categories: curriculum, instruction, assessment, and climate.

The first action is to determine an initiative whose successful implementation will increase student achievement. This is a larger goal than one of your basic administrative concerns. For example, this initiative could be driven by the district—such as the development and implementation of a course scope and sequence. This initiative could be site-based—such as the development and implementation of a data-analysis protocol whose purpose is to discover why students are achieving as they are. This initiative could be for one department or grade level—such as the use of new materials or resources (e.g., a new textbook). Or this initiative could be more specific to individual teachers' needs—such as instructional strategies that support the reading of more complex text.

> Of all the skills a principal needs to succeed, the most vital, in terms of increasing academic achievement, is that of instructional leadership.

As a principal, you can think of this as the **curriculum of the initiative.** This means you will need to know what it is, its value to students and teachers, and how you will know what implementation looks like at the highest level. This means you will need to articulate—as often as possible—the goals of the initiative to those stakeholders involved with implementation.

The second action is to determine the support for the implementation of the initiative. This support should come in a variety of professional learning opportunities—the initial instruction on the initiative, demonstrations of successful implementation within and outside of the classroom, co-planning/co-teaching sessions, collaborative meetings, and opportunities to share ideas with one another.

As a principal you can think of this support as the **instruction of the initiative.** This means you will need to develop a plan for support that takes into account the individual needs of your staff. This means you will need to articulate—as often as possible—the goals of this support to those stakeholders involved with implementation.

The third action is to determine the monitoring system for the implementation of the initiative. This monitoring must be supportive and focused on a clearly delineated set of expectations that are understood by all stakeholders.

This monitoring must include affirming and corrective feedback from a variety of sources—from you, as the leader of the initiative, from other school-site administrators, from coaches, from colleagues, and from outside experts. This monitoring must be focused on the growth of the person implementing the initiative.

As a principal, you can think of this monitoring as the **assessment of the initiative.** This means you will need to identify the timeline and process for this type of data gathering. This means you will need to articulate—as often as possible—the goals of this monitoring to those stakeholders involved with implementation.

The fourth action is to build a community of leaders. The initiative you are implementing, the support you are offering, and the success you are monitoring are too big for you to be the only leader. Thus, you need a team of stakeholders who are as dedicated to this initiative as you are.

As a principal, you can think of this community as the **climate of the initiative.** This means you must develop a plan that includes honoring and respecting the voices at your site, allows for different levels of motivation as the initiative is being implemented, and is built on the trust of all staff. This means you will need to articulate—as often as possible—the goals of this community to those stakeholders involved with implementation.

The purpose of this book is to clarify for you the actions of instructional leadership. If these actions are followed, you will be exemplifying the skills of instructional leadership, and, thus, you will be a principal who is leading a school with the stated performance outcome of increasing academic achievement for each and every student.

Leadership and Being the Boss

Before we further delineate the actions of instructional leadership, let's first define what it means to be a leader. In this book, it is clear that we believe that being a leader is the only way to successfully run a school. But not everyone sees the principal's role in this way. To many people, being the principal means being the boss.

What is the difference between being the boss and being a leader? In the simplest terms, a boss manages employees, whereas a leader inspires them to innovate, think creatively, and strive for perfection.

Based on the research, it is crucial that your staff sees you as a leader. So, think for a minute about how your staff might see you. As the boss—someone who manages their time and work? Or as a leader—someone who inspires and supports them to elevate student achievement?

From an employee's point of view, here are some differentiators between being seen as the boss or as a leader.

The Boss is in charge of an organization and its employees.	*A Leader* possesses the ability to inspire and support others to accomplish significant goals.
The BOSS . . .	A LEADER . . .
• Manages people	• Leads and supports people
• Depends on authority	• Depends on goodwill
• Drives employees	• Coaches employees
• Inspires fear	• Generates enthusiasm
• Says, "I"	• Says, "We"
• Places blame for the breakdowns	• Fixes the breakdowns
• Knows how it is done	• Shows how it is done
• Uses people	• Develops people
• Takes credit	• Gives credit
• Commands	• Asks
• Says, "Go"	• Says, "Let's go"

Table I.1: The Boss and a Leader

So, how do you think your staff sees you? If someone asked, "Who's that?" pointing to you, what do they say? "That's the boss" or "That's the leader of the school who supports my work." Don't forget that you are in control of how you are viewed by the staff, the teachers, the parents, and the students. This chart is not a checklist, something used to figure out if you are "good" or "bad." It is a tool for reflection, something that will help you think about the actions of strong leadership. So, which actions do you currently exhibit?

Obviously, being a leader is directly linked to being an instructional leader. As we have shown, the term *leadership* has many connotations, and the context in which it is used is critical. The same holds true for the term *instructional leadership*. In their review of research on how leadership influences student learning Leithwood and colleagues (2004) clearly state,

> Different forms of leadership are described in the [educational] literature using adjectives such as "instructional," "participative," "democratic," "transformational," "moral," "strategic" and the like. But these labels primarily capture different stylistic or methodological approaches to accomplishing the same two essential objectives critical to any organization's effectiveness: helping the organization set a defensible set of directions and influencing members to move in those directions. Leadership is both this simple and this complex. (p. 6)

To that end, it's important to state that when we talk about instructional leadership, we are talking about the art of inspiring a group of people toward achieving a common set of goals for learning and academic achievement.

We will be asking you to reflect on your leadership skills throughout this book. As a strong leader, you must be both reflective and self-aware. These traits are two of the most important to have if you are hoping to strengthen your leadership skills. You will determine what you do or do not want to change. We are here to provide practical solutions on how to develop instructional leadership. You are here to decide the particulars of your own growth.

> The power of leadership is not only in the ability to reflect and grow as an individual, but the ability to influence others as well.

The power of leadership lies not only in the ability to reflect and grow as an individual but in the ability to influence others as well. The research drives home that the power of leadership is in your ability to support others to grow. As Roland S. Barth (1996) articulates so well,

> The most important responsibility of every educator is to provide the conditions under which people's learning curves go off the chart. Whether one is called a principal, a teacher, a professor, a foundation official, or a parent, our most vital work is promoting human learning . . . and above all our own learning. (p. 56)

That is your task. That is the skill of instructional leadership.

A Focus on Teachers

The purpose of education, and therefore an effective principal's primary focus, is to make sure that each and every student receives the highest level of instruction every day. So, what matters most? Is it the structures of school, such as class size, retention, student placement, or summer school? Does it matter who the students are? Are educational programs the magic bullet? John Hattie (2013) called all of these things, "The Politics of Distraction—the kinds of things we talk about in our business so often, which means we avoid addressing what really matters in schools—the expertise of the teachers."

It's no surprise that the most significant effect on student achievement is caused by the classroom teacher. Time and again, research bears out that effective teachers are the most important factor contributing to student achievement. As RAND Education (2012) reminded us,

> . . . research suggests that among school-related factors, teachers matter most. When it comes to student performance on reading and math tests, a teacher is estimated to have two to three times the impact of any other school factor, including services, facilities, and even leadership. (p. 1)

Therefore, if a principal is to ensure students' academic success, they must focus on the learning of the teachers through the actions of instructional leadership.

The Spheres of Support

Consider the spheres of support as you think about your school and district. If a school or district is truly student-centered, then each educational stakeholder in the systems has very specific responsibilities. These responsibilities identify the vital, and unique, role of teachers, school-site administrators, and district-level administrators.

The vital role of teachers is to consistently and intentionally support students to own their learning. The vital role of school-site administrators is to utilize

Figure A: The Spheres of Support

instructional leadership to consistently and intentionally support teachers to own their role in student learning. The vital role of district-level administrators is to consistently and intentionally support schools-site administrators to own their role of leading initiatives that elevate student achievement.

As an administrator, you will be introducing new initiatives as needed to increase student achievement. How a teacher views an initiative is crucial—whether it be the development of a course scope and sequence, the implementation of a comprehension strategy for informational text, the use of newly adopted resources, or the collaboration inherent in a data protocol. The teacher's motivation—their understanding, their practicing, their reflecting—is key to the successful implementation of any initiative.

In other words, because your teachers are key to the implementation of any initiative that will substantively increase student achievement, you must get them to own their role in the implementation of this initiative and the learning it requires. And, you achieve this by ensuring that teachers have the authority, the capacity, and the responsibility to own their learning and to determine the most effective way for them, individually, to implement. You must support them to cultivate an ownership mindset.

> It's no surprise that the most significant effect on student achievement is caused by the classroom teacher. Time and again, research bears out that effective teachers are the most important factor contributing to student achievement.

Delegate the Authority, the Capacity, and the Responsibility

How do you support your teachers to cultivate an ownership mindset? You support them by delegating the authority, the capacity, and the responsibility to them.

Successful teachers will have the authority to make decisions regarding the day-to-day planning of their instruction. This doesn't mean that they are free to decide what they want to teach solely based on their interests. This would not prepare their students to learn skills and content needed to be college- and career-ready. Instead, this means that they have the authority to determine what they, as the teacher, need to do to support mastery of the skill by their students—for example, initial instruction, frequency and types of practice, specific opportunities for students to authentically apply their learning, and built-in opportunities for their students to transfer their learning into new situations. It is the role of the principal to ensure that teachers have the authority to make decisions about how their students will learn.

To do this, teachers must have the capacity to make the most effective and efficient decisions regarding student learning. Teachers have the capacity when they have the knowledge and skills to implement the initiative at the highest level. Teachers have the capacity when they are able to challenge themselves and self-reflect on their growth. Capacity is built by supplying teachers with the skills needed to succeed, sharing why they need them, and explaining how they will use them in current and future situations. Once teachers have the authority to make decisions about how they will teach, it is the role of the principal to ensure they have the capacity to analyze and reflect on their own learning.

Finally, teachers must have the responsibility to be held accountable for their classroom achievements. Teachers must understand their role in their students' learning and take responsibility for their successes as well as their mistakes. But they can't be held responsible if they have no understanding of what they are implementing, how they will be supported, and how they will demonstrate their learning. Principals cannot demand that teachers take responsibility if they are not given the authority and the capacity to do so.

So, how do you build authority, capacity, and responsibility within your staff? You become the model for the thinking behind ownership. You explicitly teach the skill of ownership. And, most importantly, you are willing to delegate the authority, capacity, and responsibility to your teachers.

A Framework for Instructional Leadership

This book is organized around the research, review, and reporting that delineates the features of effective instructional leadership that can improve student achievement (Leithwood et al., 2004; Vega, 2015; Vescio, Ross, and Adams, 2008; Wallace Foundation, 2013).

- "A vision of academic success for all students based on high expectations." This is the action of determining an initiative whose successful implementation will increase student achievement. **We call this the curriculum of the initiative.**

- "Support and training to promote continual professional learning." This is the action of determining the support for the implementation of the initiative. **We call this the instruction of the initiative.**

- "Data to track and promote collaborative inquiry and practices that improve student learning." This is the action of determining the monitoring system for the implementation of the initiative. **We call this the assessment of the initiative.**

- "A safe and cooperative climate for learning." This is the action of building a community of leaders. **We call this the climate of the initiative.**

These actions of instructional leadership can be organized into a framework with these four categories—curriculum, instruction, assessment, climate—and are undergirded by the understanding that all support and learning is driven by:

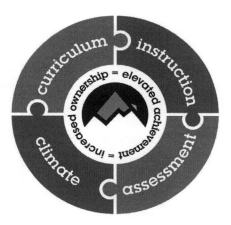

Figure B: A Learning Framework That Develops Ownership

- A clearly defined initiative with measurable and achievable outcomes.

- Highly engaging, effective, and efficient instruction.

- Regular assessment that guides decision-making.

- A positive climate.

Within this framework, we have developed a set of strategic learning practices that discretely define the support teachers need to own their learning in order to ensure successful implementation of the initiative. These practices form the foundation of the clear and consistent actions

> You become the model for the thinking behind ownership. You explicitly teach the skill of ownership. And, most importantly, you are willing to delegate the authority, capacity, and responsibility to your teachers.

the principal must take to support their teachers. In other words, these strategic learning practices translate into the actions of instructional leadership.

Although there are hundreds of actions a principal makes in a day, this book focuses on those actions in curriculum, instruction, assessment, and climate that increase the opportunities for learning—which is the basis of instructional leadership.

Chapter 1 focuses on the actions of instructional leadership in curriculum with the understanding that all support and learning is driven by a clearly defined initiative with measurable and achievable outcomes. This chapter will therefore clarify, "What is the initiative?"

In order to lead the successful implementation of an initiative, the principal needs to understand and share the answers to the following questions:

- What is the initiative?
- What is the purpose of the initiative?
- What are the success criteria of the initiative?
- How will this information be shared with the teachers?

This means that the principal must do the following:

- Clarify the goals of the initiative.
- Integrate the goals of the initiative with other expectations.
- Provide the resources needed to implement this initiative.
- Share this information with the staff.

Curriculum begins with understanding the content and skills a teacher needs to successfully implement the initiative. Curriculum must also include the demonstration of learning that shows the successful implementation of the initiative. This demonstration must be measurable and observable so that both the teacher and the principal can monitor progress. The initiative should be discussed, developed, and determined by a community of leaders. The role of the principal is to lead the implementation using the actions of instructional leadership. The use of these actions exemplifies the strategic learning practices that will be shared in this chapter.

Chapter 2 focuses on the actions of instructional leadership in instruction with the understanding that all support and learning is driven by highly engaging, effective, and efficient instruction. This chapter will therefore clarify, "How will the initiative be supported?"

In order to lead the successful implementation of an initiative, the principal needs to understand and share the answers to the following questions:

- ▸ What support will the teachers receive?
- ▸ When will the teachers receive support?
- ▸ How will the teachers work together to implement the initiative?
- ▸ How will this information be shared with the teachers?

This means that the principal must do the following:

- ▸ Clarify how the initiative will be supported and implemented.
- ▸ Establish a plan for professional learning opportunities.
- ▸ Schedule professional learning opportunities directly related to the initiative.
- ▸ Share this information with the staff.

Instruction begins with understanding that different methodologies and activities can be employed to deliver support to teachers. Because there is such a variety in the content and skills teachers need to learn, delivery can fall anywhere on the continuum from structured to open-ended. Although the decisions regarding support are the principal's to make, they must not be made without a clear understanding of the needs of each teacher—which should include input from the teacher. The role of the principal is to lead the implementation using the actions of instructional leadership. The use of these actions exemplifies the strategic learning practices that will be shared in this chapter.

Chapter 3 focuses on the actions of instructional leadership in assessment with the understanding that all support and learning is driven by regular assessment that guides decision making. This chapter will therefore clarify, "How will the initiative be monitored?"

In order to lead the successful implementation of an initiative, the principal needs to understand and share the answers to the following questions:

- ▸ How will the teachers know that they have implemented the initiative at a high level?
- ▸ How will the teachers receive feedback regarding the progress of the implementation of the initiative?
- ▸ What supports will the teachers receive if they are struggling?
- ▸ How will this information be shared with the teachers?

This means that the principal must do the following:

- ▸ Confirm the success criteria for the initiative.
- ▸ Establish a process for monitoring the implementation of the initiative.
- ▸ Establish a method for continued support for implementation.
- ▸ Share this information with the staff.

Assessment begins with understanding that the success criteria for the initiative must be concrete to both the teacher and the principal. A principal will have a difficult (if not impossible) task if the initiative does not have a clear and defined end. A teacher will struggle (if not give up) when the end is unclear or when they are unaware of what they have to do to show that they have learned. However, assessment is more than just the end or final demonstration. It also includes knowing what each step along the way looks like and how supportive each step is to the successful implementation of the initiative. The role of the principal is to lead the implementation using the actions of instructional leadership. The use of these actions exemplifies the strategic learning practices that will be shared in this chapter.

Chapter 4 focuses on the actions of instructional leadership in climate with the understanding that all support and learning is driven by a positive climate. This chapter will therefore clarify, "What is your role in the initiative?"

In order to lead the successful implementation of an initiative, the principal needs to understand and share the answers to the following questions:

- ▸ What is the teachers' role in the implementation of the initiative?
- ▸ How will the teachers support each other in the implementation of the initiative?
- ▸ How will the teachers be supported to take risks in the implementation of the initiative?
- ▸ How will this information be shared with the teachers?

This means that the principal must do the following:

- ▸ Identify the role of each stakeholder in the implementation of the initiative.
- ▸ Foster cooperation among and between stakeholders.
- ▸ Establish a plan for collaboration.
- ▸ Share this information with the staff.

Climate begins with understanding that a positive and inclusive school environment is crucial if teachers are to take risks in their learning. The positive climate determines how teachers receive feedback from the principal and their colleagues, how teachers work together to enhance one another's learning, and how teachers support one another to take risks in their learning. The role of the principal is to lead the implementation using the actions of instructional leadership. The use of these actions exemplifies the strategic learning practices that will be shared in this chapter.

The value of the actions of instructional leadership is how they work together so that a principal can successfully lead the implementation of the determined initiative. Chapter 5 is a conversation with one principal about his implementation of a hybrid learning model that includes both in-class and online learning. He shares his decision-making process in all four of the actions of instructional leadership—curriculum, instruction, assessment, and climate. This vignette shares how one principal leverages the integrative nature of these actions to more effectively and efficiently support his teachers.

Chapter 6 focuses on the individual needs of each teacher. Instructional leadership ensures that with each new initiative the teacher must be treated as a learner who must receive support specific to their needs. This still holds true for adult learners, even those who are highly educated in the schema of teaching and learning. Each learner needs to have their support differentiated in terms of how they understand the initiative, receive the support, and are held accountable.

One way to differentiate is to take into account each teacher's motivation and capacity to implement the designated initiative. For example, one teacher might have low motivation but high capacity to succeed. However, another teacher might have high motivation and low capacity. The teacher's motivation and capacity are situational and dependent on the initiative. When support is differentiated by the initiative and built to meet the individual teacher's needs, the probability for success is increased.

The role of the principal is to differentiate the support offered to each teacher, as needed, to increase the probability of a successful implementation of the initiative.

Chapter 7 focuses on the delivery of feedback that allows the teacher to take ownership of their learning. An effective principal knows that the success of any initiative begins with setting the context for teacher ownership. An effective principal also knows that each initiative must be monitored on an ongoing basis to understand how each teacher is implementing the requested action. The most effective method for a principal to monitor the teacher's work is through a question-driven process. This method of discourse allows the teacher to continue to own the process by explaining, clarifying, and reflecting on the decisions they are making to implement the initiative.

The role of the principal is to help teachers become more effective and efficient decision-makers regarding classroom practice by asking teachers how they make decisions and support metacognition through the articulation of their thinking.

Chapter 8 focuses on communication. An effective principal knows that what they say and how they say it is less important than what their teachers hear and how they hear it. Thus, one of the most important aspects of instructional leadership is to continuously, purposefully, and intentionally share information with the staff in a variety of ways. This is what we call conceptual redundancy. If teachers are to effectively implement the initiative, they deserve to hear information over and over—as many times as needed for each individual—until they clearly understand the work expected of them.

The role of the principal is not to communicate but to overcommunicate. And to overcommunicate in a way that allows each listener to hear it. If a principal wants to know if their teachers have heard the message clearly and accurately, they ask them.

How Instructional Leadership Gives You the Control

Not one of these decisions regarding curriculum, instruction, assessment, climate, differentiation, and feedback can be made in isolation. Each decision will impact other decisions. It is your job to decide how these areas work together to ensure that there is the highest likelihood of successful implementation. Your greatest power lies in your decision-making. And if your decision-making is based on the actions of instructional leadership, you will find that increased teacher ownership leads to elevated student achievement.

Let's revisit your dream school with this in mind. It is a clear example of a school where students, teachers, and administrators are all pulling together to elevate learning. Each owns their role in the process. Each is supported by another—teachers support each and every student, administration supports each and every teacher, and they all support their colleagues.

Your dream school can be a reality—and you are in control of that reality.

1 CURRICULUM

The Value of Clear Learning Expectations

When you hear the word *curriculum,* what do you think of? We bet you think of the content and skills that students or learners need to master in any given course. You also tend to think of the aim of the curriculum, the mastery of the curriculum, and the materials that support the curriculum. In terms of instructional leadership, we need to expand this definition of curriculum to refer to the content and skills that learners need to master, with the content being an initiative designed to increase student achievement, the skills being what is needed to successfully implement the initiative, and the learners as your teachers. And, just like we do with course curriculum, we need to determine the aim of the initiative, the mastery of the initiative, and the materials that support the implementation of the initiative. When we do this, we will ensure that **all support and learning is driven by a clearly defined initiative with measurable and achievable outcomes.**

The Driving Force in Curriculum

For some, the term *initiative* applies to any set of expectations that a principal wants to implement at their school site. If that is the case, then all initiatives are created equal and deserve equal priority. But research doesn't show this to be true.

> If leaders and teachers were to attain piercing clarity about what actions matter most; if we were equally clear about the value and impact of those actions; if we learned and practiced them with "simplicity and diligence" (Collins, 2001, p. 91) — something stunning would happen for our students. (Schmoker, 2016, p. 14)

The initiatives that are worth spending time on are those sets of expectations that are directly related to increasing student achievement.

Examples of Initiatives That Focus on Increasing Student Achievement

- Implementation of a new set of curriculum resources that offer students access to rigorous materials.

- Implementation of a course scope and sequence that clearly identifies those crucial skills–what the students need to know and be able to do–that ensure mastery of the content and is built to be delivered in integrated units and lessons.

- Use of an effective and efficient instructional strategy–gradual release of responsibility, reciprocal teaching, English language development (ELD) strategies, etc.–that supports learning for a diverse set of students and lends itself to metacognitive growth.

- Use of a data protocol that ensures students are adequately monitored on their growth in a specific area by focusing on those supports that were present or were missing in their instruction.

- Building student ownership for each and every student so that they can define, clarify, and lead their own learning.

- Implementation of a distance learning process that allows for student success at the same level as in-person instruction.

Table 1.1: Examples of Initiatives That Focus on Increasing Student Achievement

A student-centered initiative focused on increasing achievement inherently has a set of expectations—the criteria that clearly describe success at the highest levels. These expectations can be divided into a sequence of specific outcomes. We will use the term "outcome" in this book because a measurable and achievable outcome can be described and explained by both the principal and the teacher. If expectations are too aspirational in nature—all students will love reading by the end of third grade—the initiative is too broad, success is hard to measure, and the hard work languishes on the shore of good intentions.

> And, just like we do with course curriculum, we need to determine the aim of the initiative, the mastery of the initiative, and the materials that support the implementation of the initiative.

With any initiative thus described, there will be a learning curve for each stakeholder—especially for teachers. As Helen Timperley (2011) states,

> The central challenge faced by all leaders is to create situations that promote teacher learning about teaching practices that make a difference for students. (p. 96)

This learning curve is inevitable because the initiative should be at such a level that each teacher will be asked to develop new skills, alter current practices, support colleagues, and reflect on their implementation. This new learning must be recognized and supported by the principal because it will take time for the teachers to develop the skills necessary to implement the initiative. In other words, the principal must foster the teachers' ownership of their learning to ensure the successful implementation of the initiative.

What can a principal do to move a teacher toward owning their learning regarding the initiative? Ownership is best defined as a mindset. Teachers who know they have the authority, the capacity, and the responsibility to own their learning during this process have an ownership mindset. Thus, to support a teacher to strengthen this mindset, the principal must delegate the authority, build the capacity, and give the responsibility to each and every teacher involved in the implementation.

The Imperatives for Ownership of Curriculum

To develop ownership, several things are imperative. It is imperative for all stakeholders—principal, assistant principals, instructional coaches, and teachers—to know and be able to articulate the outcomes of the initiative that will increase student achievement. It is imperative for all stakeholders to know and be able to articulate the skills they need to learn to implement the initiative, how they will show mastery of these skills, and what successful implementation of the initiative looks like. It is imperative that they know and be able to articulate why they are implementing this initiative, what skills will support implementation, and the value of this initiative regarding increasing student achievement. It is imperative that they are provided opportunities to listen, speak, read, and write about their understanding of the initiative with colleagues. It is imperative that they know and are able to articulate where they are in the learning and implementation process—initial learning and understanding, practicing, applying, or transferring. It is imperative that each stakeholder knows and is able to articulate the resources and materials they need and how they will be used to support implementation at the highest level.

Table 1.2 below provides some helpful indicators that reveal when stakeholders are taking ownership of their learning.

How Do Stakeholders Demonstrate Ownership of Curriculum?

Each and every stakeholder is able to articulate:

- The goals of the initiative
- The purpose of the initiative
- The specific expectations of implementation
- The success criteria of the initiative
- The benefits of the initiative to students
- The benefits of the initiative to teachers
- The integration of the initiative with the other work of the school
- The resources needed to effectively implement the initiative

Table 1.2: Indicators of Ownership of Curriculum

For all stakeholders to be able to articulate the initiative they are implementing, they need to know the plan for the learning required for implementation. Thus, it is crucial for everyone to know where they are heading. While Jay McTighe and Grant Wiggins (2012) clarified the value of backward mapping for classroom learning, the same value of backward mapping holds true for adult learning.

> It is imperative that they know and be able to articulate why they are implementing this initiative, what skills will support implementation, and the value of this initiative regarding increasing student achievement.

Plan with the end in mind by first clarifying the learning you seek—the learning results . . . Then, think about the assessment evidence needed to show that students have achieved the desired learning . . . Finally, plan the means to the end—the teaching and learning activities and resources to help them achieve the goals. (p. 7)

With that in mind, principals who backward plan have the ability to tell all stakeholders what they are learning, when they are learning it, how they will apply the learning during the implementing of the initiative, and how they will continue revisiting the learning to deepen their understanding, thus giving everyone the opportunity to own their learning. All of this leads to strengthening schoolwide ownership.

Move Beyond Doing and Understanding to Owning Curriculum

What does ownership look like in practice? What does it sound like when a teacher owns their learning for the implementation of the initiative? What is the difference between a teacher who is simply *doing* the work or *understanding* the initiative and one who is *owning* what they are learning?

A teacher is *doing* when they can state the initiative.

A teacher is *understanding* when they can explain the goals and purpose of the initiative.

A teacher is *owning* what they are learning when they can state and explain the initiative as well as articulate the various aspects of the initiative, the benefits to both students and teachers, the learning that is needed for successful implementation, and the value of the initiative in terms of increasing student achievement.

The tables that follow present some examples of what this looks like and sounds like on a continuum of doing–understanding–owning in a variety of initiatives, particularly when we ask the question, "What is the initiative?"

Possible responses on the continuum from teachers working on the initiative **"Develop and implement a course scope and sequence"** *when asked,*

"What is the initiative?"

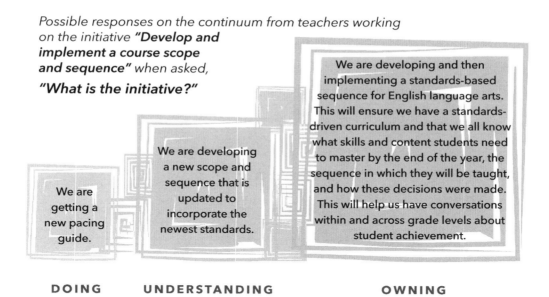

We are getting a new pacing guide.

We are developing a new scope and sequence that is updated to incorporate the newest standards.

We are developing and then implementing a standards-based sequence for English language arts. This will ensure we have a standards-driven curriculum and that we all know what skills and content students need to master by the end of the year, the sequence in which they will be taught, and how these decisions were made. This will help us have conversations within and across grade levels about student achievement.

DOING   UNDERSTANDING   OWNING

Table 1.3: Ownership Continuum of Curriculum When Developing and Implementing a Course Scope and Sequence

Possible responses on the continuum from teachers working on the initiative **"Utilize reciprocal teaching"** *when asked,*

"What is the initiative?"

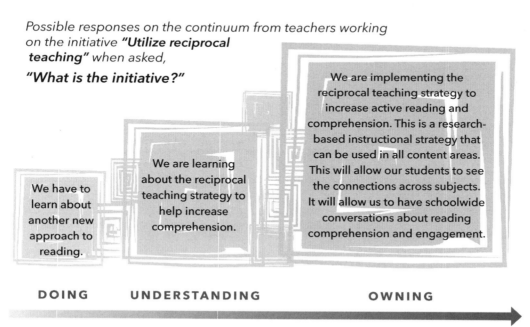

We have to learn about another new approach to reading.

We are learning about the reciprocal teaching strategy to help increase comprehension.

We are implementing the reciprocal teaching strategy to increase active reading and comprehension. This is a research-based instructional strategy that can be used in all content areas. This will allow our students to see the connections across subjects. It will allow us to have schoolwide conversations about reading comprehension and engagement.

DOING   UNDERSTANDING   OWNING

Table 1.4: Ownership Continuum of Curriculum When Utilizing a Specific Instructional Strategy, Reciprocal Teaching

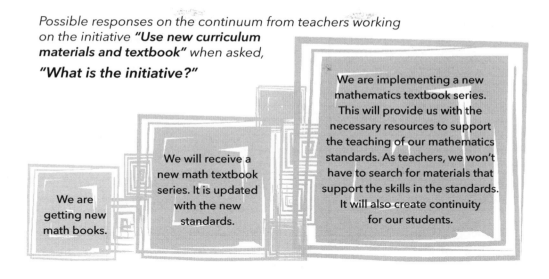

*Possible responses on the continuum from teachers working on the initiative **"Use new curriculum materials and textbook"** when asked,*

"What is the initiative?"

We are getting new math books.

We will receive a new math textbook series. It is updated with the new standards.

We are implementing a new mathematics textbook series. This will provide us with the necessary resources to support the teaching of our mathematics standards. As teachers, we won't have to search for materials that support the skills in the standards. It will also create continuity for our students.

DOING   UNDERSTANDING   OWNING

Table 1.5: Ownership Continuum of Curriculum When Using New Curriculum Materials and Textbook

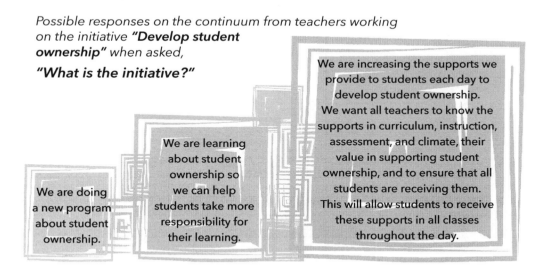

*Possible responses on the continuum from teachers working on the initiative **"Develop student ownership"** when asked,*

"What is the initiative?"

We are doing a new program about student ownership.

We are learning about student ownership so we can help students take more responsibility for their learning.

We are increasing the supports we provide to students each day to develop student ownership. We want all teachers to know the supports in curriculum, instruction, assessment, and climate, their value in supporting student ownership, and to ensure that all students are receiving them. This will allow students to receive these supports in all classes throughout the day.

DOING   UNDERSTANDING   OWNING

Table 1.6: Ownership Continuum of Curriculum When Developing Student Ownership

*Possible responses on the continuum from teachers working on the initiative **"Implement a data protocol"** when asked,*

"What is the initiative?"

We are now doing professional learning communities (PLCs).

We are meeting together to follow a data protocol that tells us whether or not our students are achieving. If not, we figure out how to reteach.

We are meeting in grade-alike and content-alike cohorts in order to follow a data protocol that will not only tell us whether or not our students are achieving but will also give us possible reasons why. We will discuss as a group and reflect on our practice, and we will share what strategies worked and what strategies didn't support our students very well. Knowing this will help ensure that our students get the best instruction possible.

DOING   UNDERSTANDING   OWNING

Table 1.7: Ownership Continuum of Curriculum When Implementing a Data Protocol

*Possible responses on the continuum from teachers working on the initiative **"Teach through distance learning"** when asked,*

"What is the initiative?"

We have to teach our students while they are at home.

We are continuing to teach our students, but the delivery, practice, and assessment process will use technology so that students can access their learning at home.

We are expecting our students to learn at levels that are as close to being in class as possible. We will utilize our current technology as we develop lessons, strategies, and assessments that can ensure at-home success. We will help parents with suggestions about how they can support their children.

DOING   UNDERSTANDING   OWNING

Table 1.8: Ownership Continuum of Curriculum When Teaching through Distance Learning

The Practices That Drive Instructional Leadership in Curriculum

Even though there are hundreds of strategies a principal could use during implementation, we will focus on the three practices in curriculum that research shows increase the opportunities for learning—by increasing the opportunities for ownership. The following three strategic learning practices are what your adult learners need in order to learn.

- **Strategic Learning Practice, Curriculum 1:** Adults are supported by relevant expectations with measurable and achievable outcomes that are accessible and drive all learning.

- **Strategic Learning Practice, Curriculum 2:** Adults are supported by a plan for learning that provides an integrated approach and that supports conceptual redundancy of the outcomes.

- **Strategic Learning Practice, Curriculum 3:** Adults are supported by access to materials that match the content and rigor of the outcomes.

Let's define each aspect of the three practices to make sure we are all on the same page.

Strategic Learning Practice, Curriculum 1: Adults are supported by **relevant expectations** with **measurable and achievable outcomes** that are **accessible** and **drive all learning**.

Relevant expectations are the actions of the initiative that clearly describe success at the highest level. These are the actions teachers need to demonstrate.

Measurable and achievable outcomes clearly define *what* teachers are expected to implement. They also define *how* teachers will demonstrate that they have successfully met the expectations. This demonstration assesses the level of application and is the measurable aspect of the outcome. The measurable outcome must be achievable in the time parameters of the initiative.

Accessible allows for all teachers to understand and articulate what they are learning, the value and purpose for learning it, and how they will know they have implemented it at the highest level.

Drive all learning implies that learning and supports link directly to the outcomes of the initiative.

Strategic Learning Practice, Curriculum 2: Adults are supported by a **plan for learning** that provides an **integrated approach** and that supports **conceptual redundancy** of the outcomes.

Plan for learning is a series of professional learning opportunities and supports that are linked together and work toward the outcome of the initiative.

Integrated approach ensures that teachers are provided multiple and varied opportunities with the expectations of the initiative. This usually includes opportunities to learn about, observe, practice, discuss, and plan specific to the expectations of the initiative.

Conceptual redundancy ensures that teachers have opportunities for repetition and practice in a variety of approaches. This also means that there is a clear connection between the goals of previous initiatives and the goals of the current initiative, all tied to student achievement.

Strategic Learning Practice, Curriculum 3: Adults are supported by access to **materials** that match the **content** and **rigor** of the outcomes.

Materials are those resources that directly support the initiative's outcome.

Content is the learning of the initiative that is to be acquired.

Rigor means materials and support exemplify the highest level of success of the initiative.

Thus, all support and learning must be driven by a clearly defined initiative with measurable and achievable outcomes because:

1. When teachers clearly understand the goal of the initiative, they have a better chance to be successful.

2. When teachers clearly understand how the work of the initiative is integrated into their current work, they have a better chance to be successful.

3. When teachers have access to appropriate and relevant resources, they have a better chance to be successful.

These practices form the foundation of the clear and consistent actions the principal must take to support their teachers' ownership of their learning to ensure successful implementation of the initiative.

How does a principal do this? They must model the thinking behind the ownership and explicitly address the skills of ownership. This takes planning. In order for all stakeholders to answer these questions—"What is the initiative?" "What is the purpose of the initiative?" and "What are the success criteria of the initiative?"—principals must be strategic in the actions they use to support staff.

In other words, these three strategic learning practices translate into the four actions of instructional leadership in curriculum:

▶ Clarify the goals of the initiative.

▶ Integrate the goals of the initiative with other expectations.

▶ Provide the resources needed to implement the initiative.

▶ ***Share this information with the staff.***

To lead the actions of curriculum, the principal must ensure that all stakeholders understand the content and skills needed to successfully implement the initiative. Curriculum must also include the demonstration of learning that shows the successful implementation of the initiative. This demonstration must be measurable and observable so that both the teacher and the principal can monitor progress. The initiative should be discussed, developed, and determined by a community of leaders. To be clear, the principal does not need to decide all of these actions by themselves—in fact, the research would argue against that. Use your faculty and staff to develop the actions of the initiative. Your task is to lead these actions.

Finally, one of the most important aspects of instructional leadership is to continuously, purposefully, and intentionally share information with the staff. This is the notion of conceptual redundancy. "To succeed, leaders must carefully select, severely limit, and then persistently clarify (and clarify, and clarify, and clarify) the work to be done by those who lead" (Schmoker, 2016, p. 11). If you think your staff needs to hear the information again, you're right and they do. If you think your staff does not need to hear the information again, you're wrong and they do.

Questions to Guide Implementing the Actions of Instructional Leadership in Curriculum

All support and learning is driven by a clearly defined initiative with measurable and achievable outcomes.

Use these planning questions to focus your support

Clarify the goals of the initiative.

❑   What are the goals of the initiative?

❑   What is the purpose of the initiative?

❑   What, specifically, will the teacher be expected to implement?

❑   What, specifically, are the success criteria for the initiative?

❑   How will the success of the initiative benefit the students?

❑   How will the success of the initiative benefit the teachers?

Integrate the goals of the initiative with other expectations.

❑   How does the initiative support the other work of the school?

Provide the resources needed to implement this initiative.

❑   What resources will the teacher need to effectively implement the initiative?

Share this information with the staff.

❑   How will this information be shared in as many distinct ways as possible?

Table 1.9: Questions to Guide Implementing the Actions of Instructional Leadership in Curriculum

An Example of Teacher Ownership in Curriculum

WHERE: A junior high school led by Principal Thompson

WHAT: The initiative is the development and implementation of a course scope and sequence (for English-language arts [ELA] in sixth, seventh, and eighth grades) that clearly identifies those crucial skills—what the students need to know and be able to do—that ensure mastery of the content and is built to be delivered in integrated units and lessons.

WHO: The seventh-grade team of three teachers

Let's hear what these teachers had to say about the initiative as they were asked these questions regarding curriculum:

▸ *What is the initiative?*

▸ *What is the purpose of the initiative?*

▸ *What are the success criteria of the initiative?*

First, we asked, *"What are you working on?"*

TEACHER 1:   "We just completed Unit 1 using our new ELA scope and sequence. We are now reviewing it to see if there are any changes we think we will need to make for this unit for next year. We are also looking at the coming units to see if we still agree with the decisions we made around the scope and sequence of the standards."

Then, *"What is the initiative you are implementing?"*

TEACHER 2:   "We were asked to develop a scope and sequence for English that was standards-based and was organized so that we could more easily plan and deliver an integrated unit. To us, that meant a unit that had a clear reading and writing focus—the reading was information to be used in the writing and the writing would be built from the text."

And, *"What is the purpose of this? What caused you all to create a new scope and sequence?"*

TEACHER 2:   "We had been looking at our ELA data to see where our students needed more support. Some standards stood out as weak areas. Once we began discussing them it became clear that we weren't all on the same page when it came to the standards—what the expectations of them were, how we were teaching them, when we were teaching them, honestly, if we were teaching them."

TEACHER 1:   "Yes. Mr. Thompson was a part of these conversations. It was clear to him that we needed to make certain we were all in agreement on the expectations of the standards and that we needed an ELA scope and sequence that was driven by the standards."

Then we asked, ***How was it decided that a scope and sequence was what was needed?***

TEACHER 3:   "In order for us to make sure our students could master the standards by the end of the year, we had to have a plan to get there. A scope and sequence allows us to map out the entire year. We made certain all our standards are taught before our high-stakes assessment. We made sure that critical standards are addressed more frequently. We made certain we built units to leverage the integrated nature of the standards. We used our learning of the standards to build a strong scope and sequence that will give our students the best opportunity to master them."

TEACHER 1:   "We also wanted to have a scope and sequence that would make certain we didn't fall into the teaching of texts. We want to make sure our instruction is driven by the standards first, using the texts as a curriculum resource to help the students learn and practice the skills of the standards."

We followed up with, ***"What are the success criteria? How will you all know that you are successful in this initiative of a standards-driven approach guided by a scope and sequence?"***

TEACHER 2:   "When we are all comfortable with the standards being the driving force of the decisions we make each day. We meet weekly to discuss what standards we focused on, how we taught them or had the students practice with them, our successes and failures, and how this will inform the decisions we make for the coming week."

TEACHER 3:   "It is amazing to me how our conversations have changed in a short period of time. The standards really drive what we do now. That was not true before. So, to answer your question, we will know we are successful when we are all teaching to the standards and when we see the increase in our student's mastery of them because of this work."

These answers show a clarity of focus that demonstrates these teachers are on their way to owning their learning when it comes to this initiative. But, how did they get here? How did Principal Thompson implement the actions of instructional leadership in curriculum?

An Example of Instructional Leadership in Curriculum

When speaking with Principal Thompson, he explained that he knew his task was to determine and lead these actions:

- ▶ Clarify the goals of the initiative.

- ▶ Integrate the goals of the initiative with other expectations.

- ▶ Provide the resources needed to implement the initiative.

- ▶ Share this information with the staff.

He began the process by answering the question from the planning chart on page 28.

- ▶ *What are the goals of the initiative?*

PRINCIPAL THOMPSON: "I was with the English teachers reviewing data from a benchmark assessment. There were some standards that the students overall did not perform well on. We began to discuss these standards. It became clear to me immediately that my teachers were not all viewing the standards in the same way. There seemed to be disagreements as to what the standards expected students to be able to do, which standards were being taught, if the standards were the instructional focus or if the text being read was the focus. The team was not on the same page at all."

"After that day, I met with the lead English teachers of each grade level and discussed my concerns. We came to an agreement that we needed to develop and implement a standards-based scope and sequence."

Once that goal had been determined, Principal Thompson then had to determine the following:

- ▶ *What is the purpose of the initiative?*

PRINCIPAL THOMPSON: "Our overall purpose is student achievement. To do that, we have to ensure we have a standards-driven curriculum. This means our teachers must know what skills the students should master by the end of the year, the sequence in which they will be taught, and how these decisions were made."

- ▶ *What, specifically, will the teacher be expected to implement?*

- ▶ *What, specifically, are the success criteria for the initiative?*

PRINCIPAL THOMPSON: "I knew I then had to decide what it was I expected from the teachers. I knew it was not enough for us to build a standards-driven scope and sequence that teachers would just follow. I knew that would lead to passive compliance. What was most important to me was that the teachers owned the scope and sequence. They needed to have a deep understanding of the standards, they needed to be able to justify the decisions made around the scope and sequence, and they needed to be able to articulate, every week, which skills they are directly teaching or supporting in each lesson, and where their students are in mastering those skills. Our success will be measured by their decisions and their ability to articulate and justify them."

But Principal Thompson knew that if he wanted real buy-in from his teachers, they would have to see the benefits to this work. He then had to determine:

> ▸ *How will the success of the initiative benefit the students?*

> ▸ *How will the success of the initiative benefit the teachers?*

PRINCIPAL THOMPSON: "I knew that if they were all stronger in the standards and we had a carefully planned scope and sequence, there would be ongoing benefits. Our teachers would be equipped with the knowledge to focus on the skills of the standards in a manner that allowed for meaningful integration. It would benefit our students to have authentic opportunities to learn, practice, and apply the skills throughout the year."

"But I know I have a range of teachers. Some are open and always looking for ways to grow. But I do have some that are quite set in their ways. If I was going to get the teachers to meet these expectations, they all had to see what was in it for them. I also knew that I couldn't lead this initiative on my own. I made certain I worked with the lead teachers to carefully craft our messaging."

"When we began to roll out the initiative, we made sure we did it in a way that honored our teachers. We asked teachers to identify the standards they felt the most confident about and to bring to our sessions examples of how they have been successful with them. Then, as we conducted the training, we had them share. The teachers all left with a much deeper understanding of the standards and were participants in the session."

"Once we developed the scope and sequence, I had the teachers develop the justification statements for the decisions they made. I knew that if my teachers could articulate how and why the decisions were made, they would own them. More importantly, they would own the thinking behind them."

"For our students, we are now confident that regardless of the class they are assigned, they will be provided with a standards-driven curriculum. Our teachers will be able to have stronger grade-level conversations and share ideas and successes. And our teachers will be able to have vertical conversations so we can more closely monitor student progress from year to year."

To ensure that his teachers did not feel overwhelmed, Principal Thompson had to determine:

▶ *How does the initiative support the other work of the school?*

PRINCIPAL THOMPSON: "Our focus last year was on the implementation of a data protocol process. I could see clearly how our work on our standards-based scope and sequence aligned beautifully to that work. But it wasn't enough that I saw it. I needed my teachers to make the connections. Rather than me telling them what I thought, I asked them. I brought out our work from last year—its goal, purpose, benefits, etc. I asked the teachers to decide if this initiative supported our previous work. If so, how? If not, why?"

"The teachers overwhelmingly saw the connections and benefits. They identified that having a scope and sequence would strengthen their data analysis. It would ensure that our focus was not on the lessons they taught but on the learning of the skills of the standards. They saw how they could expand their data conversations from just their grade level to across the grade levels. This only increased their buy-in!"

To ensure that his teachers had sufficient resources and materials to successfully implement the initiative, Principal Thompson had to determine:

▶ *What resources will the teacher need to effectively implement the initiative?*

PRINCIPAL THOMPSON: "If we are going to ask our teachers to learn something new, and possibly change the way they have been working, we had to make certain they had the right resources that would help them. We needed resources on standards, sample scope and sequences, and exemplar integrated units. We decided to utilize an outside professional development company that could help us see the standards in a new light and that could guide us through the process of developing a scope and sequence."

"We also wanted to make certain we provided them with time and support. We already had weekly grade-level PLC meetings set in our schedule.

In addition, we found dedicated time for collegial lesson study opportunities and optional additional standards training for those who felt they would benefit from it."

To ensure that his message was clearly articulated and understood, Principal Thompson had to determine:

> ▸ *How will this information be shared in as many distinct ways as possible?*

PRINCIPAL THOMPSON: "I have been working hard on being more effective with communication over the last couple of years. I learned the hard way that what I say is not always what people hear. I knew that I needed to be super redundant in my communication on every level of this initiative. This meant that things needed to be repeated over and over. And not just in one manner but in lots of ways. I also make certain I put our message in writing. This allows people to read it in their voice, and it gives them time to reflect on the message and the space to generate questions they may have."

"In addition, I make sure to work with the leadership team. First, we all have to be on the same page about how to discuss the initiative. We decide what to say and how we will share in the delivery of the message. This way, it is stated by many and heard by many."

How Other Administrators Utilize Instructional Leadership in Curriculum

INITIATIVE: Using a new math textbook

ADMINISTRATOR: Assistant principal leading the math department at a low-performing high school

"Our district adopted new math textbooks. I knew from my experiences as a teacher that this could be overwhelming. I knew that I needed to get ahead of the adoption and make certain my teachers realized that our goal was not the new textbooks. Our goal of teaching the standards remained our top priority. These new materials would just complement the work we were already doing, not replace it. I also knew that my message could conflict with what they may hear during district training sessions on the materials. So, I had to be sure to share our message over and over. It was also important that I gave them chances to state our goals as well. It could not just be me saying it.

They needed to say it in their own words as well. This made such a difference as we implemented the new materials."

INITIATIVE: Implementing a new data protocol

ADMINISTRATOR: First-year principal at an elementary school

"Our school's initiative was to implement a data protocol process. We clearly laid out the purpose of this initiative and why we believed our school was ready for it. I felt that most everyone was on board. But I knew that for this to really work we needed everyone to understand their role in the initiative. There were expectations for leadership, coaches, and teachers. There was some confusion and it felt like some folks were just going through the motions. We decided to write down what was expected from each role: what they needed to do before our data analysis meetings, what their role was during them, and what they were expected to do after each one. This took a lot of back-and-forth conversations, but the process strengthened our understanding and buy-in. I will use this process for each initiative we implement from now on."

INITIATIVE: Implementing the reciprocal teaching reading strategy

ADMINISTRATOR: CEO of a K–8 charter school

"We implemented reciprocal teaching to help strengthen our students' comprehension and engagement with text. Before we decided to focus on this initiative, we looked at the research and saw how beneficial it could be for our students. As we began the work, I started to hear some grumblings from teachers along the lines of 'this is just one more thing we need to do.' I realized that all our focus, rightly so, was on how this would support our students. I forgot to focus on how this would benefit the teachers. I had to backtrack and make certain that they all saw and believed that this would be as beneficial to them as it was to our children."

What Teachers Say About Instructional Leadership in Curriculum

INITIATIVE: Developing student ownership across the school

TEACHER: Sixth-grade teacher

"I am so appreciative of how our principal shares information regarding student ownership with us. With prior administrators, we were basically just told to show up and do this and do that. We never really knew why we were doing things and we never knew what was expected from us. With this initiative on student ownership, our principal shares with us the focus for the year, why this is our focus, what is expected from me, and what is the plan. He also tells us what we can expect from him. That way, it feels like we are a collective 'We,' not just individual 'I's."

INITIATIVE: Incorporating distance learning into instruction

TEACHER: High school chemistry teacher

"We have been told time and time again that our students should know the objective of every lesson. They should know what specific skill they are learning and how they will demonstrate that they have learned it. But when it came to our learning, we never received this before. Now we do. For every professional development session on distance learning, we are told exactly what we are expected to learn and how we will know we have learned it. We are told how the session connects to the big picture of our school goals. That clarity has been so supportive. And this has helped those of us who are still a bit uncomfortable using so much technology."

Curriculum Reflection

How well do you develop your staff to own what they are learning with regard to the initiative?

In this chapter, we have shown you what ownership looks like in practice. We have shown you what it sounds like when teachers own their part in curriculum. And we have given examples of how principals have utilized the actions of instructional leadership in order to better support the successful implementation of the selected initiative.

We have also explained the differences between teachers who are simply *doing* or *understanding* curriculum and those who are *owning* what they are learning and implementing.

Remember, we said that a teacher is *doing* when they can state the task in front of them and recite what they are doing, or what is expected of them.

Remember, we said that a teacher is *understanding* when they can explain the skills they are learning in order to successfully implement the initiative.

Remember, we said a teacher is *owning* their learning when they can articulate what skill they are learning, why they are learning it, how they will demonstrate they have learned it, and how they will use this learning to most successfully implement the initiative.

Think of your teachers and staff. When you ask them these questions, what do they say?

"What is the initiative?"

"What is the purpose of the initiative?"

"What are the success criteria of the initiative?"

Listen to their answers. Where do they fall on the doing–understanding–owning continuum? Think about the supports they need from you to develop ownership. How often and to what degree do you offer these supports? In other words, what impact do you have on leading the initiative and developing ownership?

John Hattie's research (2012) revealed that "Such passion for evaluating impact

> To lead the actions of curriculum, the principal must ensure that all stakeholders understand the content and skills needed to successfully implement the initiative.

is the single most critical lever for instructional excellence—accompanied by understanding this impact and doing something in light of the evidence and understanding" (p. viii).

What follows are reflection activities that will help you determine your impact on ownership—both areas of strength and areas of growth. These activities will help you understand how you utilize the actions of instructional leadership from the point of view of whom you are leading—the teachers and your staff.

Remember that to develop ownership, all support and learning must be driven by a clearly defined initiative with measurable and achievable outcomes.

Also, remember that your actions are key to the development of ownership and the successful implementation of the initiative.

Reflect on the Implementation of the Actions of Instructional Leadership in Curriculum

All support and learning is driven by a clearly defined initiative with measurable and achievable outcomes.

How well and how often did you clarify the goals of the initiative by offering the following supports?

- The goals of the initiative were clearly explained and defined.

- The purpose of the initiative was clearly explained and defined.

- The expectations for the teachers were clearly explained and defined.

- The success criteria for the initiative were clearly explained and defined.

- The benefits of the initiative to the students were clearly explained and defined.

- The benefits of the initiative to the teachers were clearly explained and defined.

How well and how often did you integrate the goals of the initiative with other expectations by offering the following support?

- How the initiative supports the other work of the school was clearly explained and defined.

How well and how often did you provide the resources needed to implement this initiative by offering the following support?

- The resources the teachers need to effectively implement the initiative were clearly explained and easily accessible.

How well and how often did you share the information with the staff by offering the following support?

- The information was explained, defined, and shared in as many distinct ways as possible.

Table 1.10: Narrative Reflection on the Implementation of the Actions of Instructional Leadership in Curriculum

Reflect on the Implementation of the Actions of Instructional Leadership in Curriculum

All support and learning is driven by a clearly defined initiative with measurable and achievable outcomes.

To what degree did you clarify the goals of the initiative?

- The goals of the initiative were clearly explained and defined.

5	4	3	2	1
always		sometimes		never

- The purpose of the initiative was clearly explained and defined.

5	4	3	2	1
always		sometimes		never

- The expectations for the teacher were clearly explained and defined.

5	4	3	2	1
always		sometimes		never

- The success criteria for the initiative were clearly explained and defined.

5	4	3	2	1
always		sometimes		never

- The benefits of the initiative to the students were clearly explained and defined.

5	4	3	2	1
always		sometimes		never

- The benefits of the initiative to the teachers were clearly explained and defined.

5	4	3	2	1
always		sometimes		never

To what degree did you integrate the goals of the initiative with other expectations?

- How the initiative supports the other work of the school was clearly explained and defined.

5	4	3	2	1
always		sometimes		never

To what degree did you provide the resources needed to implement this initiative?

- The resources the teachers need to effectively implement the initiative were clearly explained and easily accessible.

5	4	3	2	1
always		sometimes		never

To what degree did you share the information with the staff?

- The information was explained, defined, and shared in as many distinct ways as possible.

5	4	3	2	1
always		sometimes		never

Table 1.11: Evaluative Reflection on the Implementation of the Actions of Instructional Leadership in Curriculum

2 INSTRUCTION
The Value of Adult Learning Strategies

When you hear the word *instruction*, what do you think about? We bet you think about the strategies teachers use with their students. However, in terms of instructional leadership, instruction needs to be defined from the student's point of view—those strategies the learner will use to master the content and skills determined in curriculum.

The same holds true when *the curriculum is the initiative* and *the learner is one of your teachers*. Therefore, instruction, for a principal, is defined as those professional learning opportunities that support our teachers to learn to the highest levels. Thus, once our teachers understand what they are learning, how they will show mastery, and why they are learning, they must then determine the best way to learn. This is where you come in—you must offer your teachers a variety of ways to learn. When you do this, you will ensure that **all support and learning is driven by highly engaging, effective, and efficient instruction.**

The Driving Force in Instruction

Instructional leadership recognizes that the support for any adult expected to implement a high-stakes initiative must be engaging. That is, the teachers must want to engage in the support activities being offered. And we know from adult learning theory that adult learners will be more likely engage in such activities if they are effective and efficient. These activities must be effective—in other words, all instructional support is directly related to the goals of the initiative and the meeting of the expectations of the success criteria. These activities must be efficient—in other words, all instructional support is focused and delivered in a manner that doesn't waste anyone's time. Burns and Lawrie (2016) put it this way,

> Teacher "support" is not monolithic, but rather a multilayered array of different types of assistance that help teachers successfully transfer learning from a professional development setting to a classroom setting. (p. 2)

Therefore, the principal must also recognize that what is engaging, effective, and efficient for one teacher does not necessarily mean that it is engaging, effective, and efficient for everyone.

Examples of Instructional Supports

- **Initial Understanding:** This support delineates the purpose, goals, and expectations of the initiative along with the determined opportunities for support.

- **Initial Instruction:** This support explains the basic tenets of the initiative and offers examples of successful implementation and the sequence to get there.

- **Demonstration Lesson:** This support models the expected implementation of the initiative from an expert or someone who has successfully utilized the skills, and it should occur both outside and inside the classroom with students.

- **Observation/Feedback:** This support offers direct application of the skills in front of an expert, someone who has successfully utilized the skills, or a colleague who has begun to implement the initiative, and it includes a pre-meeting to discuss the lesson, an observation that also gathers information from students, and a debrief to discuss strengths and areas for growth.

- **Co-planning/Co-teaching:** This support allows teachers to collaborate by working together on a specific skill within the initiative, planning a lesson that one or all will teach, delivering the lesson together with clearly defined roles in the classroom, debriefing the strengths and areas for growth, taking risks in a low-stakes activity, and building trust with colleagues.

- **Lesson Study:** This support involves teachers sharing with each other their method of meeting the goals of the initiative and includes observation, discussion, planning, and reflecting.

- **Classroom Visitations:** This support allows stakeholders to observe implementation across a school or series of classrooms to determine patterns in the strengths and areas for growth.

- **Collaboration Meetings:** This support allows teachers to work together with dedicated time and focus.

Table 2.1: Examples of Instructional Supports

The most important aspect of all of this support is the opportunity for teachers to practice. In other words, teachers need a professional learning plan—not a professional development plan. A professional development plan is a series of disconnected sessions. This leads to teachers feeling that, without practice, they are expected to perfectly implement the professional development strategy the day following the session. But you and your teachers are putting together a professional learning plan—a series of instructional opportunities built to support the successful implementation of a schoolwide initiative. And this plan must include an overabundance of practice.

> Thus, once our teachers understand what they are learning, how they will show mastery, and why they are learning, they must then determine the best way to learn. This is where you come in—you must offer your teachers a variety of ways to learn.

> Leaders should have teachers overlearn best practices, too. Teachers need leaders who aren't bashful about the need to strenuously and repeatedly clarify and provide practice opportunities for teachers to learn and overlearn the fundamentals. We need to train and retrain in the most vital practices until teachers demonstrate mastery—and then periodically retrain again to ensure against forgetfulness and drift. (Schmoker, 2016, p. 22)

With any initiative focused on student growth, there will be a clearly defined set of expectations. Meeting these expectations will involve a learning curve for each stakeholder. We must pay attention to this learning curve as teachers will be asked to develop new skills, practice these new skills in a variety of situations, and identify and reflect on their strengths and areas for growth. This learning curve must be understood by the principal because it will take time for the teachers to own the skills necessary to implement the initiative at the highest level. In other words, the principal must foster the teachers' ownership of the instructional support for the initiative.

What can a principal do to move a teacher toward owning their learning regarding the skills necessary to implement the initiative at the highest level? Remember, ownership is best defined as a mindset. Teachers who know they have the authority, the capacity, and the responsibility to own how they are learning during this process have an ownership mindset. Thus, to support a teacher to strengthen this mindset, the principal must delegate the authority, build the capacity, and give the responsibility to each and every teacher involved in the implementation.

The Imperatives for Ownership of Instruction

To develop ownership, several things are imperative: It is imperative for all stakeholders—principals, assistant principals, instructional coaches, and teachers—to know and be able to articulate how they will learn the skills of the initiative that will increase student achievement. It is imperative that all stakeholders receive instructional support that will help them master the skills needed to implement the initiative at the highest level. It is imperative for them to understand how the instructional support they are receiving will help them master these skills. It is imperative that they contribute to the development of their own support plan. It is imperative that they are provided with opportunities to deepen their learning by listening, speaking, reading, and writing with their colleagues. It is imperative that each stakeholder understands their role in their own learning—that they are the masters of their own mastery.

Table 2.2 below provides some helpful indicators that reveal when stakeholders are taking ownership of their learning.

How Do Stakeholders Demonstrate Ownership of Instruction?

Each and every stakeholder is able to articulate:

- The goals and success criteria of the initiative
- The instructional supports teachers will receive to achieve the goals of the initiative
- The purpose and value of each of these instructional supports
- The expectations of each type of support
- The process of asking for and receiving additional support
- The purpose and value of working with colleagues on implementation of the initiative
- The power of being able to contribute ideas to the implementation plan
- The timeline and plan for the initiative, which include milestones for the learning

Table 2.2: Indicators of Ownership of Instruction

If all stakeholders are able to articulate the points in the above chart effectively, they are engaging in the process of metacognition. Metacognition is a learner's ability to think about their own thinking, to know what they are thinking, and to learn about their own learning—in other words, metacognition is cognition about cognition. Allen Newell (1990) identifies two aspects of metacognition: (1) knowledge about cognition and (2) regulation of cognition. Helen Timperley (2011) says,

> It is imperative that all stakeholders receive instructional support that will help them master the skills needed to implement the initiative at the highest level.

> It is much more important that the activities were directly relevant to achieving the goals of professional learning and of building relevant knowledge and understanding of the ideas both theoretically and in practice than the form of the activity. (p. 65)

Thus, the strongest strategies that we can have teachers engage in are those that support their learning and that can be applied to push their learning in future endeavors. These strategies must also be directly linked to the successful implementation of the initiative—all of which leads to strengthening schoolwide ownership.

Move Beyond Doing and Understanding to Owning Instruction

What does ownership look like in practice? What does it sound like when a teacher owns their part in the instruction of the initiative? What is the difference between a teacher who is simply *doing* the work or *understanding* the initiative and one who is *owning* how they are learning?

A teacher is *doing* when they can state the activities they are expected to participate in.

A teacher is *understanding* when they can explain the goals and purpose of each of the instructional supports they are participating in.

A teacher is *owning* how they are learning when they can articulate the opportunities for instructional support and explain the purpose of each support, the benefits of these supports to the high-level implementation of the initiative, and the benefits of these supports to their own growth as an educator.

The tables that follow present some examples of what this looks like and sounds like on a continuum of doing–understanding–owning in a variety of initiatives, particularly when we ask the question, "How will the initiative be supported?"

*Possible responses on the continuum from teachers working on the initiative **"Develop and implement a course scope and sequence"** when asked,*

"How will the initiative be supported?"

We must go to three PD sessions on the standards.

We are going to have PD on the standards. This will help us develop a new scope and sequence.

We will all be trained in a better understanding of the standards. From there we will develop a scope and sequence. We will participate in weekly meetings and collegial lesson study opportunities as we implement the new scope and sequence. Additional standards training and coaching will be provided as needed. We will receive feedback on our progress from administration and the colleague or coach we work with on lesson study. There will be monthly all-ELA staff meetings to share progress on the implementation of the scope and sequence across all grades/courses.

DOING   **UNDERSTANDING**   **OWNING**

Table 2.3: Ownership Continuum of Instruction When Developing and Implementing a Course Scope and Sequence

*Possible responses on the continuum from teachers working on the initiative **"Utilize reciprocal teaching"** when asked,*

"How will the initiative be supported?"

We have after-school sessions on a new reading strategy that we must attend.

We are having professional development sessions and instructional coaching about a new reading strategy called reciprocal teaching. It will help our students with their reading comprehension.

We will be trained in the reciprocal teaching process. We will participate in demonstration lessons that will include a planning meeting, observation, and debrief session led by an instructional coach. We will have a collegial partner to support through monthly lesson study sessions. These sessions will allow for planning, collegial observations, and debrief sessions. We will participate in vertical and horizontal department meetings to share the impact reciprocal teaching is having on student comprehension and engagement.

DOING   **UNDERSTANDING**   **OWNING**

Table 2.4: Ownership Continuum of Instruction When Utilizing a Specific Instructional Strategy, Reciprocal Teaching

*Possible responses on the continuum from teachers working on the initiative **"Use new curriculum materials and textbook"** when asked,*

"How will the initiative be supported?"

A representative from the company is going to train us on our new math books.

We are going to attend sessions about our new math series and how it supports the math standards. This will happen a couple of times this year.

We will be trained on the standards, the adopted scope and sequence, and the new mathematics textbook program. We will meet weekly in course-alike clusters to plan and share successes and challenges. Quarterly sessions by the textbook company will be provided to deepen the understandings of the available resources and to answer questions. The school selection committee will present to the entire school staff and parents to share why this textbook program was chosen and how it supports the school's vision of mathematics instruction.

DOING **UNDERSTANDING** **OWNING**

Table 2.5: Ownership Continuum of Instruction When Using New Curriculum Materials and Textbook

*Possible responses on the continuum from teachers working on the initiative **"Develop student ownership"** when asked,*

"How will the initiative be supported?"

We have a session. Then we must go to other teachers' classrooms to observe them.

We are going to focus on student ownership this year. We will be learning about it first so we can practice some of the strategies in our classrooms. Then we will see how each of us is doing as we visit classrooms.

We will all be trained in the strategic learning practices to develop student ownership. We will participate in facilitated classroom walks to observe these supports in action. We will be participating in an ongoing book study on developing student ownership. Each of us will be paired up with a colleague to participate in a lesson study focused on student ownership. Demo lessons and additional coaching will be provided as needed.

DOING **UNDERSTANDING** **OWNING**

Table 2.6: Ownership Continuum of Instruction When Developing Student Ownership

Possible responses on the continuum from teachers working on the initiative **"Implement a data protocol"** when asked,

"How will the initiative be supported?"

We will attend a professional development session on the use of this protocol. At our first attempt to implement the protocol, our instructional coach will lead us through it. At the end of this meeting, we will reflect and discuss the positives and challenges of working together. We will then decide, as a team, what support we need next. I am thinking that I will need support on how to be more vulnerable with other teachers.

We have a set schedule that allows us to meet once a month for an extended period of time. We follow the protocol and plan reteaching lessons together.

We learned about it at one of our staff meetings.

DOING　　　　**UNDERSTANDING**　　　　**OWNING**

Table 2.7: Ownership Continuum of Instruction When Implementing a Data Protocol

Possible responses on the continuum from teachers working on the initiative **"Teach through distance learning"** when asked,

"How will the initiative be supported?"

Our main task is to develop lessons that allow students to continue learning at high levels. We meet with our team and with the instructional coach weekly. We develop an online lesson and then deliver it to one of our classes while our colleagues observe. Afterward, we discuss the strengths of and gaps in the instruction. The next week, we do it again with another lesson and another teacher. This process gives us lots of chances to practice with feedback and to get new strategies from each other.

We have online support for the new technology. We also meet every two weeks with grade-level colleagues to discuss and develop lessons and assessments.

We attended a session on how to use the new technology at home.

DOING　　　　**UNDERSTANDING**　　　　**OWNING**

Table 2.8: Ownership Continuum of Instruction When Teaching through Distance Learning

The Practices That Drive Instructional Leadership in Instruction

Although there are hundreds of strategies a principal could use during implementation, we will focus on the three practices in instruction that research shows increase the opportunities for learning—by increasing the opportunities for ownership. The following three strategic learning practices are what your adult learners need in order to learn.

- **Strategic Learning Practice, Instruction 1:** Adults are supported by opportunities for meaningful engagement using structured learner-to-learner communication.

- **Strategic Learning Practice, Instruction 2:** Adults are supported by opportunities for meaningful engagement using highly effective instructional strategies.

- **Strategic Learning Practice, Instruction 3:** Adults are supported by opportunities for meaningful engagement where instructional time is used efficiently.

Let's begin by defining each aspect of the three practices.

Strategic Learning Practice, Instruction 1: Adults are supported by **opportunities** for **meaningful engagement** using **structured learner-to-learner communication**.

Opportunities are those occasions for teachers to be actively engaged. The higher the quantity and the higher the quality of these opportunities, the higher the probability of learning.

Meaningful engagements are those times when teachers are involved in interactions that directly lead to increased understanding or mastery of the expectations of the initiative.

Structured implies that these interactions have a purpose, a value, and a goal. These interactions can be planned by the principal or the teachers, but everyone should be clear on their role in the interaction.

Learner-to-learner communication is an interaction between teachers in which each has an opportunity to push their thinking and understanding of the initiative expectations through speaking and listening.

Strategic Learning Practice, Instruction 2: Adults are supported by **opportunities** for **meaningful engagement** using highly **effective instructional strategies**.

Opportunities are those occasions for teachers to be actively engaged. The higher the quantity and the higher the quality of these opportunities, the higher the probability of learning.

Meaningful engagements are those times when teachers are involved in interactions that directly lead to increased understanding or mastery of the expectations of the initiative.

Effective implies that the teachers demonstrate the intended outcome at the end of the time allotted.

Instructional strategies are all the approaches an instructional leader may employ to engage his or her teachers in meeting the outcomes of the initiative. These instructional strategies consider both the outcome and the adults who are learning.

Strategic Learning Practice, Instruction 3: Adults are supported by **opportunities** for **meaningful engagement** where **instructional time** is used **efficiently**.

Opportunities are those occasions for teachers to be actively engaged. The higher the quantity and the higher the quality of these opportunities, the higher the probability of learning.

Meaningful engagements are those times when teachers are involved in interactions that directly lead to increased understanding or mastery of the expectations of the initiative.

Instructional time is the time allotted for each professional development opportunity or support.

Efficiently is the least amount of time required for the highest rate of learning. Nonproductive time is kept to a minimum.

Thus, all support and learning must be driven by highly engaging, effective, and efficient instruction because:

1. When teachers have opportunities for meaningful engagement using structured learner-to-learner communication, they have a better chance to be successful.

2. When teachers have opportunities for meaningful engagement using highly effective instructional strategies, they have a better chance to be successful.

3. When teachers have opportunities for meaningful engagement where instructional time is used efficiently, they have a better chance to be successful.

These practices form the foundation of the clear and consistent actions the principal must take to support their teachers' ownership of their learning to ensure successful implementation of the initiative.

How does a principal do this? They must model the thinking behind the ownership and explicitly address the skills of ownership. This takes planning. In order for all stakeholders to answer these questions—"What support will teachers receive?" "When will teachers receive support?" and "How will teachers work together to implement the initiative?"—principals must be strategic in the actions they use to support staff.

In other words, these three strategic learning practices translate into the four actions of instructional leadership in instruction:

▸ Clarify how the initiative will be supported and implemented.

▸ Establish a plan for professional learning opportunities.

▸ Schedule professional learning opportunities directly related to the initiative.

▸ *Share this information with the staff.*

To lead the actions of instruction, the principal must ensure that all stakeholders understand the different methodologies and activities that can be employed to deliver support to the teacher. Because there is such variety in the content and skills teachers need to learn, delivery can fall anywhere on the continuum from highly structured to more open-ended. These supports should be discussed, developed, and determined by a community of leaders. Even though the decisions regarding support are the principal's to make, be certain you do so with a clear understanding of the needs of each teacher—and include input from the teacher during decision-making. Use your faculty and staff to develop the actions of support for the initiative. Your task is to lead these actions.

In addition, it is worth repeating that one of the most important aspects of instructional leadership is to continuously, purposefully, and intentionally share information regarding support with the staff. Schmoker (2016) says,

> . . . to bring out the best in employees, leaders must meticulously craft every communication—every goal and directive—and then check with employees to make sure that they properly understood the message. Clarity is essential to productive action. (p. 19)

This is the notion of conceptual redundancy. If you think your teachers need to hear about the instructional support plan again, you're right and they do. If you think your teachers do not need to hear about the instructional support plan again, you're wrong and they do.

Questions to Guide Implementing the Actions of Instructional Leadership in Instruction

All support and learning is driven by highly engaging, effective, and efficient instruction.

Use these planning questions to focus your support.

Clarify how the initiative will be supported and implemented.

❑   What supports will the teacher receive in order to achieve the goals of the initiative?

Establish a plan for professional learning opportunities.

❑   What is the expectation of the teacher for each provided support?

❑   How will teachers ask for and receive additional support?

❑   How will the teachers work together to implement the initiative?

❑   How will the teachers have opportunities to contribute ideas to the implementation plan?

Schedule professional learning opportunities directly related to the initiative.

❑   What is the timeline and plan for the initiative?

❑   When will the teachers receive support?

❑   What are the milestone expectations for each learner?

Share this information with the staff.

❑   How will this information be shared in as many distinct ways as possible?

Table 2.9: Questions to Guide Implementing the Actions of Instructional Leadership in Instruction

An Example of Teacher Ownership in Instruction

WHERE: An elementary school led by Principal Washington

WHAT: The initiative is the implementation of the metacognitive reading strategy of reciprocal teaching for upper grades (third, fourth, fifth, and sixth grades) that clearly teaches those reading skills—questioning, clarifying, summarizing, and predicting—that lead to stronger comprehension of informational text.

WHO: The fourth-grade team of five teachers

Let's hear what these teachers had to say about the initiative as they were asked these questions regarding instruction:

▶   *What support will the teachers receive?*

TEACHER 1:   "The first support was the professional development session by an outside company. The presenter was knowledgeable and had lots of good strategies that would work with our diverse student body. During the training, we practiced the talk groups so that we got a feel for what the kids would be doing. We also received lots of specific ways to teach questioning, clarifying, summarizing, and predicting."

TEACHER 2:   "I am most excited about seeing a demo lesson. The presenter will be back in the school in a few weeks to put my students into the reciprocal teaching group for the first time. My task in the meantime is to teach the students each of the four skills. I also am reminding them of the norms we use when we work together. They can't wait until they get to work in the groups."

TEACHER 3:   "I am a bit more sequential and I look at how Mrs. Washington laid out the entire plan that included different options for support. We started with the initial presentation. Then, I will observe the demo lesson in Teacher B's room. After that, I will have an opportunity to try the groups out on my own or with the presenter setting them up. Soon after that, the presenter will return and observe each of us to give us pointers on our progress. We will continue to meet as a grade-level team to discuss how it is going. We also have the option to teach a lesson together. I don't know if I will do that, but I am happy to know it is a choice."

▶   *When will the teachers receive support?*

TEACHER 3:   "Mrs. Washington is very methodical about how she rolled out the support for implementation. We had the initial training in August before school started. We are now using the month of September to teach the four skills. In a few weeks, we will observe the demo lesson for the talk group. Toward the end of October, we will each be observed by the presenter and have a chance to talk about our progress and next steps. After that, we will determine individually what we need for support. Even though Mrs. Washington observes the process, she let us know that she doesn't expect to see consistent use of the strategy until January. That alleviates a lot of stress for me."

TEACHER 4:   "The timeline is perfect. This gives us a chance to practice, practice, practice. We know we are going to make mistakes and the principal is okay with that—in fact, she says she wants us to report the mistakes to each other so that we can learn from each other."

> *How will the teachers work together to implement the initiative?*

TEACHER 5:   "We have dedicated grade-level meetings once a month. We will have a chance to share our experiences with the strategy. Our principal also will get us sub coverage so that we can work with each other and share our strengths. I have a nice way that I teach summarizing that I will share with the team. Teacher B has an effective way she sets up groups and group norms. She says she's willing to come into our classes and teach each group of students. I can't wait."

TEACHER 2:   "Getting into each other's classrooms is the most fun. Seeing how my colleagues approach the same job as me is eye-opening. We all do it differently. This lets us honor how we are different but all working toward the same outcome. It also lets me steal ideas from everyone."

These answers show clarity of focus that demonstrates these teachers are on their way to owning their learning when it comes to this initiative. But, how did they get here? How did Principal Washington implement the actions of instructional leadership in instruction?

An Example of Instructional Leadership in Instruction

When speaking with Principal Washington, she explained that she knew her task was to determine and lead these actions:

- ► Establish a plan for professional learning opportunities.
- ► Clarify how the initiative will be supported and implemented.
- ► Schedule professional learning opportunities directly related to the initiative.
- ► Share this information with the staff.

She began the process by answering the questions from the planning chart on page 55.

> ► *What supports will the teacher receive in order to achieve the goals of the initiative?*

PRINCIPAL WASHINGTON: "Because the learning needed to successfully have students working together to make meaning from text is so complex, I knew that my teachers needed a variety of supports and time to practice. The initial support opportunities were fairly standard for every teacher but then become individualized once they determine their own needs. The process is straightforward. First, everyone would attend a full-day session on the what, why, and how of reciprocal teaching. Next, each teacher will have an opportunity to observe the students working in groups using the strategy. This demonstration lesson will include a meeting beforehand and a debrief afterward. If requested, other teachers could have a demo lesson with their students. Each teacher will have an opportunity to be observed with feedback. We have a plan that all of this support would be from an outside provider and I have budgeted for this. After everyone participates in this plan of support, we will begin to individualize. The teachers themselves will let me know what support they need to meet the expected outcomes."

Once the variety of supports had been determined, Principal Washington then had to determine the following:

> ► *What is the expectation of the teacher for each provided support?*
>
> ► *How will teachers ask for and receive additional support?*
>
> ► *How will the teachers work together to implement the initiative?*
>
> ► *How will the teachers have opportunities to contribute ideas to the implementation plan?*

PRINCIPAL WASHINGTON: "It depends on the support. At the initial session, the expectation is that the teachers will gather as much information as possible and begin thinking about how they will implement this strategy in their class. Before the demo lesson, the expectation is that the teachers will have taught their students how to question, clarify, summarize, and predict, along with developing group work norms. After the demo lesson, the expectation is that the teachers will put their students into reciprocal teaching talk groups at least once a week, but we are recommending more. From there, the expectation is that the teachers will determine their strengths and areas for growth and develop their own individualized plan."

"Asking for additional support is a challenge for my teachers because they want to be perfect the first time they do anything. I remind them that this is a learning process and that mistakes will be made. With the team, we developed a support request form that the teacher can use to ask for help. It includes the area of need, how they want the support, and who they want to support them. Because they meet regularly, they discuss the different options open to them."

"The teachers will work together during their monthly grade-level meetings. They have two meetings a month and the second one is always focused on the implementation of reciprocal teaching. During this time, they share their progress and difficulties. They also can request sub time to work together to co-plan and co-teach. I am of the mindset, if they want to work together, I will do anything in my power to find them the time. This is also how they use the support request form."

"The initial plan was developed with contributions from a leadership team pulled from fourth-, fifth-, and sixth-grade teachers. After we determined the need—low reading scores with information text—and the solution—the use of reciprocal teaching, we then brainstormed what they would need to implement this strategy within their classrooms. That is how we determined the first part of the support with the outside provider. After that, the teachers will then have a say in their own plan and determine their next steps."

Principal Washington knew that she wanted to ensure focus on the initiative, so all of the support must be related to the initiative. She wasn't willing to pull her teachers off the task. So, she then had to determine:

▶ *What is the timeline and plan for the initiative?*

▶ *When will the teachers receive support?*

▶ *What are the milestone expectations for each learner?*

PRINCIPAL WASHINGTON: "The timeline is pretty simple. Once we decided on reciprocal teaching as the initiative for the year, we knew we would start the year with the initial session. The overall timeline was that the teachers would have the fall semester for the students to learn and practice reciprocal teaching. The expectation was that students would then be able to apply and transfer the strategy throughout the winter and spring."

"Given this timeline, the bulk of the structured support occurred in the fall. After that, the support becomes individualized depending on the needs of the teacher and the students."

"The milestone expectations were built off of the larger timeline. The largest milestone is in January when the students should be able to effectively and efficiently make meaning from text using reciprocal teaching. The milestone for teachers before then is sequenced. By October, the students will have been taught the four skills of questioning, clarifying, summarizing, and predicting. By the end of October, the students will have experienced the talk group. In November and December, the students will practice the talk group at least once a week. By the time January comes around, they will be proficient in using this comprehension strategy. The next milestones occur in the spring when the students are expected to transfer this skill into all content areas. By May, the expectation is that students will make meaning from any type of text, reflect on their growth, and explain their process for deeper reading."

To ensure that her message was clearly articulated and understood, Principal Washington had to determine:

> ► *How will the information be shared in as many distinct ways as possible?*

PRINCIPAL WASHINGTON: "Sharing the information regarding support for reciprocal teaching was actually quite easy. Because we had developed the support plan together, my task was to remind them of our decisions. Before every session, I ask the group two questions: What are the goals of the initiative? How will today's session support the implementation of the initiative? We discuss and make sure we are all on the same page. I do this before each session—even those I don't participate in. At the end of those days, I send the teachers who participated an email and ask them to reflect on the work: What did you learn? How will this help you implement the initiative? What are your next steps? I always end the emails with a reminder that they can request any support they feel they need. And I try my hardest to provide it for them."

How Other Administrators Utilize Instructional Leadership in Instruction

INITIATIVE: Developing student ownership

ADMINISTRATOR: Principal of an elementary school

"Our school initiative is to develop greater student ownership. This initiative is comprehensive and impacts all teachers. We first developed our end goal of what student ownership should look and sound like at every grade level, K–5. We then developed our benchmark goals and a year-long plan designed to reach our benchmarks and end goal. Having this plan at the onset allowed me to do two very important things. First, it allowed me to make certain I had a budget in place to support the plan. Second, it allowed us all to see and understand the plan from day 1. There have been times in the past when I started with our first step and then planned along the way. I figured I would see how we were doing and then just decide the next step. This was not successful. Sometimes, I ran out of money. But more importantly, the teachers, the ones implementing the initiative, didn't even know what the plan was. This approach of an upfront, transparent plan allows us all to know exactly where we are headed and our plan to get there. We are in it together from day 1."

INITIATIVE: Implementing a mathematics course scope and sequence

ADMINISTRATOR: Assistant principal of a high school

"Our mathematics department is implementing new scope and sequences that map out our math standards and mathematical practices for each course. We are expecting our teachers to plan and implement lessons that balance both the content and the metacognition of the practices every day. For many of our teachers, this is a great shift in how they plan and teach. We know that they will need a lot of practice and varied support. I have a Malcolm Gladwell quote in my office. It says, 'Practice isn't the thing you do once you're good. It's the thing you do that makes you good.' I know the importance of practice and yet too often we do not provide our teachers with the time, space, and support to practice. We made sure our plan included lots of support and opportunities to practice and grow along the way."

INITIATIVE: Teaching through distance learning

ADMINISTRATOR: Principal of a middle school

"Our initiative is to implement a distance learning program for ELA and mathematics. Like many schools, we have a wide range of ability levels when it comes to technology and distance learning strategies. At the onset of our initiative, we conducted a survey to assess where each teacher was. We looked at their competencies in all areas of our initiative. We found that we had teachers who were either weak or strong in all areas. But then we also had teachers with mixed levels of skills. We decided that our plan to support the initiative had to allow for differentiation. We decided that we would create modules for each part of the initiative. From there we used the data we gathered from the survey and developed individual learning plans for each teacher. Teachers have access to all modules if they want to go outside of their individual plan, but each was assured that they would receive the specific supports they needed."

What Teachers Say About Instructional Leadership in Instruction

INITIATIVE: Implementing new science textbooks

TEACHER: Eighth-grade Earth science teacher

"We got a new textbook program this year. Last year we built a scope and sequence from the new science standards. This year our initiative is to implement the new textbook program following our scope and sequence. There are a lot of print and online resources that the program comes with. In previous new textbook adoptions, we usually attended a district-provided full-day training session on the program. These days were overwhelming and many of us would leave uncertain how to use the materials. This time our principal worked with us to develop a plan that would give us support throughout the year. We started with an overview of the program. From there we will have shorter sessions that focus on a particular component of the program. We then are provided with planning time to decide how we could incorporate that component into our instruction. Giving us the year to really understand the materials and ongoing support has made all of the difference."

INITIATIVE: Implementing data protocol process

TEACHER: Tenth-grade English-language arts teacher

"We are implementing a data protocol process. As an ELA department, we are analyzing student writing samples from each unit and our quarterly benchmark assessments. This process will allow us to not just look at the data but to analyze the instructional decisions we made that impacted the data so we can replicate strong practices and rectify areas of need. As we reviewed the plan of support for the year with the principal, we noticed that there were going to be additional needs. The plan did not include training on scoring writing. We need this if we were to be calibrated. It did not include the time needed to score writing. It included our grade-level PLC time, but we felt we needed to have department PLC time as well so we could have vertical conversations on student performance. Thankfully, we saw the plan at the onset and were able to share these needs with the principal. She had not budgeted for this, but she was able to move money around so that we could have the best plan possible to successfully implement our initiative."

Instruction Reflection

How well do you develop your staff to own how they are learning with regard to the initiative?

In this chapter, we have shown you what ownership looks like in practice. We have shown you what it sounds like when teachers own their part in instruction. And we have given examples of how principals have utilized the actions of instructional leadership in order to better support the successful implementation of the selected initiative.

We have also explained the differences between teachers who are simply *doing* or *understanding* instruction and those who are *owning* how they are learning and implementing.

Remember we said that a teacher is *doing* when they can state the activities they are expected to participate in.

Remember we said that a teacher is *understanding* when they can explain the goals and purpose of each of the instructional supports they are participating in.

Remember we said a teacher is *owning* how they are learning when they can articulate the opportunities for instructional support and explain the purpose of each support, the benefits of these supports to the high-level implementation of the initiative, and the benefits of these supports to their own growth as an educator.

Think of your teachers and staff. When you ask them these questions, what do they say?

"What support will the teachers receive?"

"When will the teachers receive support?"

"How will the teachers work together to implement the initiative?"

Listen to their answers. Where do they fall on the doing–understanding–owning continuum? Think about the supports they need from you to develop ownership. How often and to what degree do you offer these supports? In other words, what impact do you have on leading the initiative and developing ownership?

John Hattie's research (2012) revealed that "Such passion for evaluating impact is the single most critical lever for instructional excellence—accompanied by understanding this impact and doing something in light of the evidence and understanding" (p. viii).

What follows are reflection activities that will help you determine your impact on ownership—both areas of strength and areas of growth. These activities will help you understand how you utilize the actions of instructional leadership from the point of view of who you are leading—the teachers and your staff.

> To lead the actions of instruction, the principal must ensure that all stakeholders understand the different methodologies and activities that can be employed to deliver support to the teacher.

Remember that to develop ownership, all support and learning must be driven by highly engaging, effective, and efficient instruction.

Also, remember that your actions are key to the development of ownership and the successful implementation of the initiative.

Reflect on the Implementation of the Actions of Instructional Leadership in Instruction

All support and learning is driven by highly engaging, effective, and efficient instruction.

How well and how often did you clarify how the initiative will be supported by offering the following supports?

- The instructional supports teachers needed in order to achieve the goal of the initiative were clearly explained and offered.

How well did you establish and how often did you clarify the plan for professional learning opportunities by offering the following support?

- The expectations for the teachers were clearly explained and defined.

- How the teachers ask for and receive additional support was clearly explained and offered.

- How the teachers work together to implement the initiative was clearly explained and offered.

- How the teachers have opportunities to contribute ideas to the implementation plan was clearly explained and offered.

How well and how often did you schedule professional learning opportunities directly related to the initiative by offering the following support?

- The timeline and plan for the initiative was clearly explained and defined.

- When the teachers receive support was clearly explained and defined.

- The milestone expectations for each learner were clearly explained and defined.

How well and how often did you share the information with the staff by offering the following support?

- The information was explained, defined, and shared in as many distinct ways as possible.

Table 2.10: Narrative Reflection on the Implementation of the Actions of Instructional Leadership in Instruction

Reflect on the Implementation of the Actions of Instructional Leadership in Instruction

All support and learning is driven by a highly engaging, effective, and efficient instruction.

To what degree did you clarify how the initiative will be supported?

- The instructional supports teachers needed in order to achieve the goal of the initiative were clearly explained and offered.

5	4	3	2	1
always		sometimes		never

To what degree did you clarify the plan for professional learning opportunities?

- The expectations for the teachers were clearly explained and defined.

5	4	3	2	1
always		sometimes		never

- How the teachers ask for and receive additional support was clearly explained and offered.

5	4	3	2	1
always		sometimes		never

- How the teachers work together to implement the initiative was clearly explained and offered.

5	4	3	2	1
always		sometimes		never

- How the teachers have opportunities to contribute ideas to the implementation plan was clearly explained and offered.

5	4	3	2	1
always		sometimes		never

To what degree did you schedule professional learning opportunities directly related to the initiative?

- The timeline and plan for the initiative was clearly explained and defined.

5	4	3	2	1
always		sometimes		never

- When the teachers receive support was clearly explained and defined.

5	4	3	2	1
always		sometimes		never

- The milestone expectations for each learner were clearly explained and defined.

5	4	3	2	1
always		sometimes		never

To what degree did you share the information with the staff?

- The information was explained, defined, and shared in as many distinct ways as possible.

5	4	3	2	1
always		sometimes		never

Table 2.11: Evaluative Reflection on the Implementation of the Actions of Instructional Leadership in Instruction

3 ASSESSMENT
The Value of Monitoring Learning Strategies

When you hear the word *assessment,* what do you think of? We bet you think of the tools teachers use to determine what a student knows or doesn't know and the tools you use to evaluate teachers. In fact, for many, being assessed and being evaluated means the same thing. Teachers tend to look at anything to do with monitoring as negative. That's because the usual scenario has the principal sitting in a classroom, observing what is going on, and then making statements regarding what the teacher did well and what they need to change before the next evaluation. This scenario only focuses on the summative. There is no formative support. In other words, this process is assessment *of* learning, not assessment *for* learning.

This typical approach to assessment tends to make the principal the focus— they are the final judge of what teachers know or don't know, do or don't do. We need to flip this to make the teacher the focus—they are the judge of their own knowledge and skills. True ownership begins when the principal looks at assessment from the point of view of the teacher. That is assessment *for* learning and therefore can support evidence-based decision-making. When we do this, we will ensure that **all support and learning is driven by regular assessment that guides decision-making.**

The Driving Force in Assessment

Assessment, when viewed through the lens of instructional leadership, is defined as the teacher's ability to understand when they are learning and when they are struggling. This understanding directly relates to the learning needed to implement the initiative (determined in curriculum) and to the professional learning opportunities to support implementation (as determined in instruction), and it is an essential component in determining the success of the initiative. Stronge (2006) reinforces this premise in his research on performance evaluation systems for professional support personnel:

> Therefore, if established goals (for both individual teacher and the school) are to be achieved, an emphasis on improvement and monitoring of progress toward goal accomplishment is inherent in a sound evaluation system. (p. 6)

In other words, once a teacher knows what they are learning, how they will learn it, and how they will show they have learned it, they can then identify— every step of the way—if they are learning and if they are struggling. They will better understand the data that tells them whether they are learning or struggling. This means teachers know the value of consistent monitoring of their implementation of the initiative. They know the principal is just checking for understanding of their progress. This also means teachers know when they need to ask for more support. Your role is to support them on this journey.

This redefined approach to assessment includes the gathering of lots of formative data. You have to do more than just check to see if the teacher is doing what has been asked. You need to gather data that tells you how the teacher is approaching the initiative, their understanding of the value, purpose, and expectations of the initiative, their strong points and their struggles with implementation, and their thinking about how to incorporate the initiative into their teaching.

In other words, you need to gather data about how they make decisions. You do this by observing how they make decisions regarding what to teach, how to teach, whether or not students are learning, how to offer feedback—both affirming and corrective—and how to build a respectful, cooperative, and collaborative classroom.

But an observation only takes you so far. We must use this data and then talk to the teacher about how they made decisions. As Stronge (2006) said,

> A teacher evaluation system that is designed for school improvement and teacher growth can improve teaching. The value in evaluation is improving performance. At its most fundamental level,

Examples of Types of Classroom Monitoring

- **Drop-In:** An administrator pops into the classroom for less than 5 minutes to check in and see how things are going. The purpose of this observation is to be seen by teachers and students, to take a quick pulse on the school for that day and time, and to be available for any questions.

- **Walk Through:** An administrator or a small team of leaders enters a classroom for no less than 7 minutes (up to 15 minutes) looking for specific criteria related to the initiative, which the teacher knows beforehand. This observation might include talking to students and getting their input, reading the walls and student work, and observing how the teacher operates as the lead in the classroom. The purpose of this observation is to gather data that allows you to look at trends and patterns across a school or department or grade level that will help you determine next support opportunities.

- **Formative Observation:** An administrator observes an entire lesson for no less than 30 minutes looking for specific criteria related to the initiative. The purpose of this observation is to discover how the teacher is making decisions about their implementation of the initiative. The principal will observe the actions and words of the teacher, talk with students, and review student work. As the principal is gathering data, they are also writing down the questions that will lead the debrief session. The debrief session occurs as soon as possible after the observation and offers the teacher an opportunity to explain the metacognitive decision-making for that lesson.

- **Evaluation:** An administrator observes the teacher using the required time commitment and criteria as set out from the district evaluation process. The strength of a formal evaluation is when the criteria can be linked directly to the initiative criteria.

Table 3.1: Examples of Types of Classroom Monitoring

teacher evaluation helps teachers identify the need to improve and then serves as a catalyst for accomplishing those desired improvements. If teacher evaluation is to serve this important function, then there must be a mechanism for communicating why and how to change. (p. 17)

The conversation is when the real learning—both for the teacher and the principal—happens. The discussion is the mechanism for communicating why and how to change. In other words, the principal must foster the teachers' ownership of the assessment support for the initiative.

What can a principal do to move a teacher toward owning their learning regarding monitoring when they are learning and when they are struggling? Remember, ownership is best defined as a mindset. Teachers who know they have the authority, the capacity, and the responsibility to own how they are learning during this process have an ownership mindset. Thus, to support a teacher to strengthen this mindset, the principal must delegate the authority,

> True ownership begins when the principal looks at assessment from the point of view of the teacher. That is assessment for learning and therefore can support evidence-based decision-making.

build the capacity, and give the responsibility to each and every teacher involved in the implementation.

The Imperatives for Ownership of Assessment

To develop ownership, several things are imperative: It is imperative for all stakeholders—principals, assistant principals, instructional coaches, and teachers—to know and be able to articulate the success criteria of the initiative. It is imperative for all stakeholders to know and be able to articulate when they are meeting the goals of the criteria and when they are struggling. It is imperative for them to identify those supports that helped them learn. It is imperative that they also identify when they are struggling and find the support they need to continue learning. It is imperative that they accept feedback as a means for learning and that they offer feedback to others. It is imperative that each stakeholder engages in reflective practices to clarify, understand, and deepen their own learning.

Table 3.2 provides some helpful indicators that reveal when stakeholders are taking ownership of their learning.

What Graham Nuthall (2007) says about student-centered assessment applies to teacher-centered assessment:

> Learning, of whatever kind, is about change, and unless you know what has changed in the minds, skills, and attitudes of your students, you cannot really know how effective you have been. (p. 35)

How Do Stakeholders Demonstrate Ownership of Assessment?

Each and every stakeholder is able to articulate:

- The goals of the initiative
- The success criteria of the initiative
- The monitoring process for the implementation of the initiative
- The method for receiving feedback during the monitoring process
- The timeline for receiving feedback during the monitoring process
- The manner in which teachers identify success and struggles
- The manner in which to receive supports if they are struggling
- The process for contributing to their own individual learning plan

Table 3.2: Indicators of Ownership of Assessment

Therefore, if all stakeholders are monitoring their implementation of the initiative and can articulate the points above, they can effectively use what they are learning to make decisions that impact student achievement.

As a principal utilizing instructional leadership, you need to know what has changed in the minds, skills, and attitudes of your teachers. However, you cannot know what has changed in the minds, skills, or attitudes of your teachers unless the teachers are part of the process—unless teachers own their role in identifying when they are learning and when they are struggling. As explained in chapter 2, the value of learner-centered assessment is fo___

research around metacognition and the regulation of cognitio___

> It is imperative for all stakeholders to know and be able to articulate when they are meeting the goals of the criteria and when they are struggling.

To the greatest extent possible, monitoring shou___
itive and productive process. We can ensure___
on practices that teachers have had ample___
and rehearse until they reach master___
monitoring should mostly consis___
progress and increased consi___
ties to complement prac___

Thus, the task of the principal is to integrate the teachers into the monitoring plan so that they are willing participants in the metacognitive process—all of which leads to strengthening schoolwide ownership.

Move Beyond Doing and Understanding to Owning Assessment

What does ownership look like in practice? What does it sound like when a teacher owns their part in the assessment of the initiative? What is the difference between a teacher who is simply *doing* the work or *understanding* the initiative and one who is *owning* how well they are learning?

A teacher is *doing* when they can state how they will finish the work being asked of them.

A teacher is *understanding* when they can explain how they know they are learning and effectively implementing the skills of the initiative.

A teacher is *owning* how well they are learning when they articulate if they are learning or struggling and why, what to do if they need more support, how participating in a reflective conversation builds their skills, and how assessing their learning helps them learn more and at a deeper level.

The tables that follow present som⸻ ⸻hat this looks like and sounds like on ⸻ ⸻ng in a variety of initiatives, ⸻e initiative be monitored?"

⸻nd in the
⸻.
⸻d be a pos-
⸻this by focusing
⸻opportunity to learn
⸻. Under these conditions,
⸻ of capturing and celebrating
⸻tency, with plenty of opportuni-
⸻tioners." (Schmoker, 2016, p. 24)

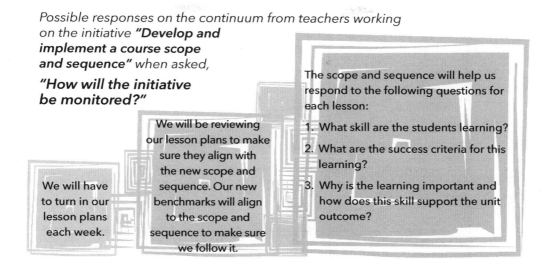

*Possible responses on the continuum from teachers working on the initiative **"Develop and implement a course scope and sequence"** when asked,*

"How will the initiative be monitored?"

We will have to turn in our lesson plans each week.

We will be reviewing our lesson plans to make sure they align with the new scope and sequence. Our new benchmarks will align to the scope and sequence to make sure we follow it.

The scope and sequence will help us respond to the following questions for each lesson:

1. What skill are the students learning?

2. What are the success criteria for this learning?

3. Why is the learning important and how does this skill support the unit outcome?

DOING   **UNDERSTANDING**   **OWNING**

Table 3.3: Ownership Continuum of Assessment When Developing and Implementing a Course Scope and Sequence

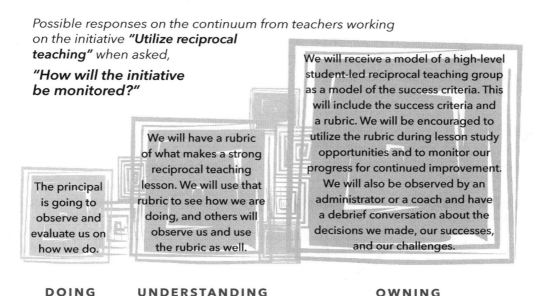

*Possible responses on the continuum from teachers working on the initiative **"Utilize reciprocal teaching"** when asked,*

"How will the initiative be monitored?"

The principal is going to observe and evaluate us on how we do.

We will have a rubric of what makes a strong reciprocal teaching lesson. We will use that rubric to see how we are doing, and others will observe us and use the rubric as well.

We will receive a model of a high-level student-led reciprocal teaching group as a model of the success criteria. This will include the success criteria and a rubric. We will be encouraged to utilize the rubric during lesson study opportunities and to monitor our progress for continued improvement. We will also be observed by an administrator or a coach and have a debrief conversation about the decisions we made, our successes, and our challenges.

DOING   **UNDERSTANDING**   **OWNING**

Table 3.4: Ownership Continuum of Assessment When Utilizing a Specific Instructional Strategy, Reciprocal Teaching

Possible responses on the continuum from teachers working on the initiative **"Use new curriculum materials and textbook"** when asked,

"How will the initiative be monitored?"

We will have to follow the pacing guide using the textbook.

We will work with our teammates to plan using the textbook and then turn in our lessons for review.

We will develop weekly mathematics lesson plans that follow the scope and sequence and utilize the mathematics textbook. Teachers will participate in a lesson study with a colleague to support their planning and implementation. Teachers will use this process to articulate their decisions on which instructional resources from the textbook they chose, which they adapted, and why. Optional demonstration lessons will be offered as needed.

DOING   UNDERSTANDING   OWNING

Table 3.5: Ownership Continuum of Assessment When Using New Curriculum Materials and Textbook

Possible responses on the continuum from teachers working on the initiative **"Develop student ownership"** when asked,

"How will the initiative be monitored?"

We are going to be observed and scored.

We will work with a colleague and an outside expert to implement the practices. We will use the exemplars to check against how we are doing.

We will receive exemplars of a high level of student ownership in the areas of curriculum, instruction, assessment, and climate. We will use these exemplars to support planning and reflection. We will be encouraged to monitor their progress against the exemplars for continued improvement. We will participate in a lesson study with a colleague and an outside expert who will be driven by pre- and post-observation conversations about the decisions we made, our successes, and our challenges.

DOING   UNDERSTANDING   OWNING

Table 3.6: Ownership Continuum of Assessment When Developing Student Ownership

Possible responses on the continuum from teachers working on the initiative **"Implement a data protocol"** *when asked,*

"How will the initiative be monitored?"

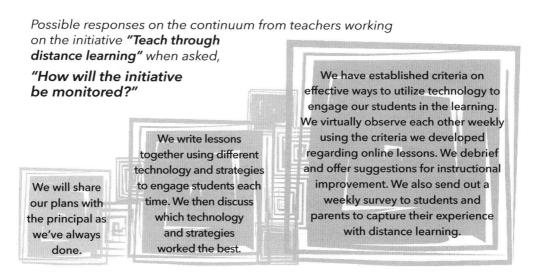

We will share our reteaching plans with the principal.

We will work together to write our reteaching lessons. We will share our meeting notes with the principal and explain how we used this information to craft our reteaching lessons.

The team will work together to follow the protocol and take substantive notes on each aspect. We will use these notes to then craft the reteaching lessons necessary to support our students. We will reflect on the process. However, the implementation of this protocol is what begins the next meeting. The team will review our plans and the successes and challenges of our students. We will identify what worked and what needs improvement. We are held accountable to each other by making our decisions transparent.

DOING   UNDERSTANDING   OWNING

Table 3.7: Ownership Continuum of Assessment When Implementing a Data Protocol

Possible responses on the continuum from teachers working on the initiative **"Teach through distance learning"** *when asked,*

"How will the initiative be monitored?"

We will share our plans with the principal as we've always done.

We write lessons together using different technology and strategies to engage students each time. We then discuss which technology and strategies worked the best.

We have established criteria on effective ways to utilize technology to engage our students in the learning. We virtually observe each other weekly using the criteria we developed regarding online lessons. We debrief and offer suggestions for instructional improvement. We also send out a weekly survey to students and parents to capture their experience with distance learning.

DOING   UNDERSTANDING   OWNING

Table 3.8: Ownership Continuum of Assessment When Teaching through Distance Learning

The Practices That Drive Instructional Leadership in Assessment

Although there are hundreds of strategies a principal could use during implementation, we will focus on the three practices in assessment that research shows increase the opportunities for learning—by increasing the opportunities for ownership. The following three strategic learning practices are what your adult learners need in order to learn.

- **Strategic Learning Practice, Assessment 1:** Adults are supported by data that is used to monitor current understanding and provide feedback.

- **Strategic Learning Practice, Assessment 2:** Adults are supported by data that is used to monitor current understanding and adjust as needed.

- **Strategic Learning Practice, Assessment 3:** Adults are supported by data that is used to differentiate based on predetermined needs.

Let's begin by defining each aspect of the three practices.

Strategic Learning Practice, Assessment 1: Adults are supported by **data** that is used to **monitor current understanding** and **provide feedback**.

Data is any information that is gathered to indicate whether the teachers are meeting the expectations of the initiative. This data can be an informal conversation with a teacher or an observation of practice.

Monitor assumes the instructional leader is constantly and consistently checking to see if teachers are having success or are struggling.

Current understanding refers to the intended expectation at that specific moment in the initiative.

Provide feedback is information that is communicated to the teacher to affirm, clarify, or redirect their learning.

Strategic Learning Practice, Assessment 2: Adults are supported by **data** that is used to **monitor current understanding** and **adjust** as **needed**.

Data is any information that is gathered to indicate whether the teachers are meeting the expectations of the initiative. This data can be an informal conversation with a teacher or an observation of practice.

Monitor assumes the instructional leader is constantly and consistently checking to see if teachers are having success or are struggling.

Current understanding refers to the intended expectation at that specific moment in the initiative.

Adjust implies modifying the professional development or supports for those who are struggling or to accelerate the pace for those who are succeeding more quickly than anticipated.

As needed implies that the instructional leader utilizes the information from the monitoring to determine whether or not to adjust.

Strategic Learning Practice, Assessment 3: Adults are supported by data that is used to **differentiate** based on **predetermined needs**.

Data is any information that is gathered to indicate if the teacher has any specific concerns that could impact success in meeting the initiative expectations.

Differentiate is to adapt or modify instructional materials, instructional strategies, or instructional processes to meet the specific needs of specific teachers so that the teachers can be supported in meeting the initiative outcome.

Predetermined needs include all the data an instructional leader is privy to before planning the professional development and supports for the initiative. This could include a teacher's experience, evaluations, skill, or will.

Thus, all support and learning must be driven by regular assessment that guides decision-making because:

1. When teachers clearly understand the data that is used to monitor current understanding and provide feedback, they have a better chance to be successful.

2. When teachers clearly understand the data that is used to monitor current understanding and adjust as needed, they have a better chance to be successful.

3. When teachers clearly understand the data that is used to differentiate based on their individual needs, they have a better chance to be successful.

These practices form the foundation of the clear and consistent actions the principal must take to support their teachers' ownership of their learning to ensure successful implementation of the initiative.

How does a principal do this? They must model the thinking behind the ownership and explicitly address the skills of ownership. This takes planning.

In order for all stakeholders to answer these questions—"How will the teachers know that they have implemented the initiative at a high level?" "How will the teachers receive feedback regarding the progress of the implementation of the initiative?" and "What supports will the teachers receive if they are struggling?"—principals must be strategic in the actions they use to support staff.

In other words, these three strategic learning practices translate into the four actions of instructional leadership in assessment:

- Confirm the success criteria of the initiative.

- Establish a method for monitoring the implementation of the initiative.

- Establish a method for continued support of implementation.

- ***Share this information with the staff.***

To lead the actions of assessment, the principal must ensure that all stakeholders understand the success criteria for the successful implementation of the initiative. A principal will have a difficult (if not impossible) task if the initiative does not have a clear and defined end. A teacher will struggle (if not give up) when the end is unclear or when they are unaware of what they have to do to show that they have learned. Thus, the success criteria must be concrete for all stakeholders—principal, assistant principal, instructional coach, and teacher. But the role of instructional leadership in assessment is more than just evaluating the end or final demonstration—it includes knowing what each step looks and sounds like along the way, offering affirming and corrective feedback, giving multiple opportunities for practice, and allowing for additional time and resources. Your task is to lead these actions.

And remember, you must continuously, purposefully, and intentionally share assessment information with the staff. Clarity is key to success. In his book about organizational health, Patrick Lencioni (2012) conveys the importance of clarity this way:

> . . . there is no way that their employees can be empowered to fully execute their responsibilities if they don't receive clear and consistent messages about what is important from their leaders across the organization. (pp. 74–75)

This is the notion of conceptual redundancy. If you think your teachers need to hear the information again, you're right and they do. If you think your staff does not need to hear the information again, you're wrong because they do.

Questions to Guide Implementing the Actions of Instructional Leadership in Assessment

All support and learning is driven by regular assessment that guides decision-making.

Use these planning questions to focus your support.

Confirm the success criteria for the initiative.

❑ What are the success criteria of the initiative?

❑ How will the teachers know that they have implemented the initiative at a high level?

Establish a method for monitoring the implementation of the initiative.

❑ How will the teachers receive feedback regarding the progress of the implementation of the initiative?

❑ When will teachers receive feedback regarding the progress of the implementation of the initiative?

Establish a method for continued support of implementation.

❑ How will the teachers identify when they are succeeding and when they are struggling?

❑ What supports will the teachers receive if they are struggling?

❑ How will the teachers have a say in determining their needs?

Share this information with the staff.

❑ How will this information be shared in as many distinct ways as possible?

Table 3.9: Questions to Guide Implementing the Actions of Instructional Leadership in Assessment

An Example of Teacher Ownership in Assessment

WHERE: A comprehensive high school led by Principal Sanchez

WHAT: The initiative is to increase the supports teachers provide to students daily that develop student ownership and lead to elevated academic achievement.

WHO: All teachers

Let's hear what these teachers had to say about the initiative as they were asked these questions regarding assessment:

> ▸ *How will the teachers know that they have implemented the initiative at a high level?*

> ▸ *How will the teachers receive feedback regarding the progress of the implementation of the initiative?*

> ▸ *What supports will the teachers receive if they are struggling?*

First, we asked, *"What is the initiative you are implementing?"*

TEACHER 1:   "We are increasing the supports we provide our students to develop student ownership."

Then, *"Why student ownership? How did you determine that this was an important initiative for your school?"*

TEACHER 2:   "We are a fairly high-performing school. We have a lot of students who have done well since they began school. But we noticed that for many of our students, they are focused just on their grades. They want to complete the assignments and get the grade. They aren't really engaging in the work or willing to struggle. They just want to get the right answer and move on."

TEACHER 1:   "So we are working on how we can support them to own more of their role in their learning. We have identified 12 research-based practices that support student ownership. We are incorporating them into our classrooms, as appropriate, to support our students."

And, *"What is your end goal? How will you know you have successfully supported students to own their learning?"*

TEACHER 3:   "Our end goal is for our students to be able to tell us about their learning. We have three questions that we are now constantly posing to our students. Our questions are:

- What are you learning?

- How will you use this learning in the future?

- How will you demonstrate that you have learned it?"

TEACHER 2:   "We have also developed a continuum from weaker answers to stronger answers. We are constantly monitoring to see if more students are providing stronger answers. Then we are reflecting on why. What did we do, or not do, to support them?"

TEACHER 1:   "Our ultimate goal is for our kids to not only answer at a strong level but to understand and value why knowing this supports them as learners. This is information they should demand as learners."

Next we asked, ***"You mentioned that you are monitoring your student responses along the way and reflecting on the supports you offered. How are you being supported? Does anyone provide you with feedback on how you're doing?"***

TEACHER 1:   "Yes. We realized as we began this initiative that if we wanted our students to change, we had to change. And change can be hard, especially if you are trying to do it on your own. We have set up a collegial lesson study process. We work with a colleague and discuss our lesson plan—what we are intentionally focusing on regarding the 12 practices. We talk about why we chose these supports for this lesson and how they will support the students in ownership. Then our colleague watches as the lesson is taught. They also talk to the kids and ask our questions as well as just discuss ownership with them. Afterward, we talk about the lesson. We discuss where we are seeing growth and why. We talk about where we want to get stronger and how. We just share ideas and push each other's thinking."

Our follow-up, ***"That sounds like a great process. How did you prepare yourselves to have these types of conversations?"***

TEACHER 2:   "This was a big part of our training. We worked with an outside company that first modeled the process for us. We learned a lot about the difference between feedback and advice. We wanted to be sure that our conversations were just that, conversations. We are not there to give our colleague advice. We want to be 'feeding back' to them what we saw. So, I may say to my colleague something like this, 'I noticed that you had the students pair up and discuss the strategy before you had them start. How did you decide to do that?' I genuinely want to understand her thinking and decision-making. This type of conversation makes us both stronger."

TEACHER 1:   "Don't get us wrong. This has taken a lot of work and practice. It wasn't what we were used to. But it has been so helpful to us. It has even changed how I give feedback to my students."

We responded, *"It sounds like things are going well. What about your colleagues who may be struggling? Those who aren't seeing progress?"*

TEACHER 2:   "Ms. Sanchez has offered us lots of other supports. We have the option to attend additional training on the practices that support student ownership. We have also been asked to open our classrooms, if we are comfortable, so teachers can come by to observe and talk to our students. This lets us get ideas and approaches from others."

TEACHER 3:   "Yes. I also found this helpful because I saw some of my students in other classrooms. Some were taking greater ownership in other classrooms than they were in mine. I realized that the only difference was me. I needed to support them more."

These answers show clarity of focus that demonstrates these teachers are on their way to owning their learning when it comes to this initiative. But, how did they get here? How did Principal Sanchez implement the actions of instructional leadership in assessment?

An Example of Instructional Leadership in Assessment

When speaking with Principal Sanchez, she explained that she knew her task was to determine and lead these actions:

▸ Confirm the success criteria of the initiative.

▸ Establish a method for monitoring the implementation of the initiative.

▸ Establish a method for continued support of implementation.

▸ Share this information with the staff.

She began the process by answering the questions from the planning chart on page 81.

▸ *What are the success criteria of the initiative?*

PRINCIPAL SANCHEZ: "We will know we are successful when our students take a larger role in owning their learning. For us, this means that our students understand and value the importance of always knowing what they are learning, why they are learning it, and how they will know when they have learned it. But we have some benchmarks we need to hit along the way if we want to reach this goal. We know that if we want to get to the students, we will need to go through the adults. So, we have to make sure our teachers understand and believe in the value of student ownership. That we all have a shared understanding of what it is, and what it looks and sounds like at the highest level. They must know the research-based practices that support student ownership—what they are, how they support student ownership, and what they look like when they are successfully implemented. For us to meet these benchmarks, I have to know along the way what my teachers are thinking. I need to know where they are in meeting the benchmarks, how they got there or didn't, and what specific supports they will need to continue to grow."

Once success criteria have been determined, Principal Sanchez then had to determine the following:

> ▸ *How will the teachers know that they have implemented the initiative at a high level?*

PRINCIPAL SANCHEZ: "When we began this initiative, we had a lot of conversations and professional learning sessions on student ownership and the practices that support it. I thought that we left these sessions with the same ideas. But as I began to have follow-up conversations with teachers, it became clear to me that we were internalizing the information differently. That is when I knew we had to codify our understandings. Together, we have developed and put in writing what student ownership would look and sound like at the highest level for us. We have created a continuum from where we currently are to that highest level, knowing that this is about growth. We have also developed an initiative message. This message explains why we are focusing on student ownership, what the value of it is to our students, and what the value is to the adults who support our students. We revisit this message at the onset of every meeting on student ownership."

Principal Sanchez knew that the monitoring must allow for growth. She then determined:

> ▸ *How will the teachers receive feedback regarding the progress of the implementation of the initiative?*

> ▸ *When will teachers receive feedback regarding the progress of the implementation of the initiative?*

PRINCIPAL SANCHEZ: "Feedback is an area that I have been working on as a principal. All the research supports the impact feedback has on learning. We discuss it with our teachers all the time regarding students receiving quality feedback. But we often fall short when it comes to adults receiving feedback. So, I knew that if I was going to ask teachers to change, they had to be supported with consistent and relevant feedback. I also knew that I could not do that alone. We have had training as a campus on feedback. It was important that we differentiated between giving advice and 'feeding back.' We do this through a question-driven process. I see my role as supporting my teachers to make stronger decisions. I can only do this if I understand how they make their decisions. It is easy to observe someone, draw conclusions, and offer advice. But change happens when we support them to own the process. Question-driven discourse allows them to explain, clarify, and reflect on the decisions they are making to impact student ownership."

"We have built several tiers of monitoring and feedback support. Each teacher is asked to self-reflect and share where they are in the process and their steps for continued growth. Our teachers all participate in a collegial lesson study process that allows them to provide each other with feedback and support. In addition, our administration team conducts planned observations that are scheduled to include an immediate question-driven conversation. These conversations allow us to then reflect as an administration team to capture where our teachers are in the process, what supports are having the greatest impact, and where additional supports may be needed."

But Principal Sanchez knew that she wanted to ensure that the support was focused on individual teacher growth and that the teachers needed to feel active in the process. So, she then had to determine:

> ▸ *How will the teacher identify when they are succeeding and when they are struggling?*
>
> ▸ *What supports will the teachers receive if they are struggling?*
>
> ▸ *How will the teacher have a say in determining their needs?*

PRINCIPAL SANCHEZ: "I feel that as an administration team, we have a pretty good handle on who is succeeding and who is struggling. But we want the teachers to own their role in their own learning in this initiative. The self-reflection and question-driven feedback process have helped us a lot in this area. Our teachers are self-assessing against the continuum we developed. They are establishing their next steps and then utilizing the collegial lesson study as a safe place to practice and get feedback. Our conversations with teachers after observations have given them a chance to reflect on their decisions and identify what is having an impact and where they may need to make changes. But, even with all of that, we do have teachers that are not as self-reflective or haven't really bought into the initiative. For these individuals I have developed a differentiated plan that I work through with them."

"We knew that when we began this initiative that it was going to take a lot of support and that we would have to differentiate. There are aspects of our plan that we rolled out at the beginning of the initiative that were for all stakeholders. We then built in optional supports that teachers could utilize as they choose. And for those on a differentiated plan, we offered some required next steps. These included additional training on student ownership and the practices that support it. Some teachers just needed more time to grapple with the content, some needed the redundancy of hearing it again, and some needed to begin implementing it and then go back and learn deeper. We have asked teachers to open their classrooms so others could observe what supports they are offering students and to see how students react to those supports. We also have identified some teachers who are have shown great success and paired them up with teachers who are struggling. They are being asked to share what decisions they are making, why they make them, and the impact they are seeing on their students."

"I won't lie. It has been a lot of work to implement and monitor this initiative. We are seeing real growth in our students. I believe because this initiative impacts every classroom they are in, they are getting tremendous support throughout their day. And I have to say, I have never seen teachers take greater ownership of their own learning."

To ensure that her message was clearly articulated and understood, Principal Sanchez had to determine:

> ▸ *How will the information be shared in as many distinct ways as possible?*

PRINCIPAL SANCHEZ: "I shared earlier how I realized that we internalize information differently. Knowing this, I could not just share the plan and hope that everyone would hear it the same way. Codifying our initiative and success criteria helped us tremendously to ensure that we were in agreement. I have shared a copy of it with every teacher and I bring this out in every feedback session. We always start our conversation by reviewing it. I know it is important that we always keep the context and goal in mind."

How Other Administrators Utilize Instructional Leadership in Assessment

INITIATIVE: Implementing a learning management system

ADMINISTRATOR: Principal at a suburban high school

"Our school is implementing a learning management system (LMS) that will allow us to build and manage instruction online and for our students that are learning from home. When we spoke to the company of the LMS, they offered us training on the system. But the training included a couple of sessions that all teachers would receive. As I observed and spoke with teachers, it was clear that some required additional support. We had to negotiate to get a more differentiated plan. This could not be a one-size-fits-all solution. I have some quite tech-savvy teachers who would acclimate quickly, and I have others who are somewhat tech-phobic. I knew we had to have a plan that considered our varying needs and that allowed everyone to be successful. If the teachers cannot effectively utilize the LMS, our students would suffer."

INITIATIVE: Implementing a new early literacy program for K–2

ADMINISTRATOR: Principal of an elementary school

"We recently implemented a new early literacy program for our primary grades. We wanted to support our teachers with research-based resources to build foundational literacy skills. The program is quite comprehensive and included a lot of bells and whistles. We set up a year-long plan that included monthly training sessions on the materials to ensure that our teachers were comfortable with the purpose and suggested uses of each component so we could effectively use them as needed. About three months in, the teachers let me know that they were very comfortable with the program materials. This was substantiated during my classroom visits and conversations with teachers. The teachers were using the materials effectively, and we were seeing some initial gains in our early literacy diagnostic data. We decided to cancel the remaining training sessions and instead use that time for further collegial planning and data analysis."

INITIATIVE: Implementing a data analysis protocol

ADMINISTRATOR: Assistant principal of an upper elementary school

"We recently implemented a data analysis protocol process at our school. I lead the fifth-grade team. I knew that I wanted to be present during their PLC sessions as well as with individual teachers. We must find the time to listen to where teachers are in implementing the process and be sure that we ask strong questions to help clarify their thinking and that we provide relevant feedback. I was initially struggling to find dedicated time for this, yet I knew it was instrumental to our success. I utilized a time tracker app and began to capture my actions every day. It allowed me to discover where I was spending my time. I then moved my more administrative tasks over to others and freed up time to support the teachers in conversations driven to support their daily decisions. I learned more about where they were finding success and where they needed support during these times."

What Teachers Say About Instructional Leadership in Assessment

INITIATIVE: Developing a social sciences course scope and sequence

TEACHER: Eleventh-grade government teacher

"We recently developed a standards-based scope and sequence for our courses. It allowed us to plan the entire year and develop meaningful unit prompts so students could demonstrate their collective learning. I felt confident going into the first unit. My assistant principal did an observation of one of my lessons and was asking me some good questions about my lesson and how it was tied to the unit outcome. I struggled to articulate the connections and realized they were not there. And if they weren't there for me, they certainly were not there for my students. The conversation helped me realize that I needed to revisit the unit plan and make certain I could see how it all connected."

INITIATIVE: Using inquiry-based science instruction

TEACHER: Seventh-grade science teacher

"I came from a school that used inquiry-based instruction. I am very confident in this approach to science instruction. Our school was just beginning this process. I had a conversation with our principal once he rolled out our initiative and professional development plan. After sharing my experience, discussing my planning approach, and having him observe some lessons, I requested a varied plan for my professional development. I wanted to take more of a leadership role and support teachers in making the transition. He allowed this to happen. It was a much better use of my time rather than starting at square one with everyone else. And I was able to share with them the successes and failures I had along the way. Supporting them and articulating my planning and delivery has made me a stronger teacher as well."

Assessment Reflection

How well do you develop your staff to own how well they are learning in regard to the initiative?

In this chapter, we have shown you what ownership looks like in practice. We have shown you what it sounds like when teachers own their part in assessment. And we have given examples of how principals have utilized the actions of instructional leadership in order to better support the successful implementation of the selected initiative.

We have also explained the differences between teachers who are simply *doing* or *understanding* assessment and those who are *owning* how well they are learning and implementing.

Remember, we said that a teacher is *doing* when they can state how they will finish the work being asked of them.

Remember, we said that a teacher is *understanding* when they can explain how they know they are learning and effectively implementing the skills of the initiative.

Remember, we said a teacher is *owning* how well they are learning when they articulate if they are learning or struggling and why, what to do if they need more support, how participating in a reflective conversation builds their skills, and how assessing their learning helps them learn more and at a deeper level.

Think of your teachers and staff. When you ask them these questions, what do they say?

"How will the teachers know that they have implemented the initiative at a high level?"

"How will the teachers receive feedback regarding the progress of the implementation of the initiatives?"

"What supports will the teachers receive if they are struggling?"

Listen to their answers. Where do they fall on the doing–understanding–owning continuum? Think about the supports they need from you to develop ownership. How often and to what degree do you offer these supports? In other words, what impact do you have on leading the initiative and developing ownership?

John Hattie's research (2012) revealed that "Such passion for evaluating impact is the single most critical lever for instructional excellence—accompanied by understanding this impact and doing something in light of the evidence and understanding" (p. viii).

What follows are reflection activities that will help you determine your impact on ownership—both areas of strength and areas of growth. These activities will help you understand how you utilize the actions of instructional leadership from the point of view of whom you are leading—the teachers and your staff.

> To lead the actions of assessment, the principal must ensure that all stakeholders understand the success criteria for the successful implementation of the initiative. A principal will have a difficult (if not impossible) task if the initiative does not have a clear and defined end.

Remember that to develop ownership, all support and learning must be driven by regular assessment that guides decision-making.

Also, remember that your actions are key to the development of ownership and the successful implementation of the initiative.

Reflect on the Implementation of the Actions of Instructional Leadership in Assessment

All support and learning is driven by regular assessment that guides decision-making.

How well and how often did you confirm the success criteria for the initiative by offering the following supports?

- The success criteria of the initiative were clearly explained and defined.

- How the teachers know that they have implemented the initiative at a high level was clearly explained and defined.

How well did you establish and how often did you clarify the method for monitoring the implementation of the initiative by offering the following support?

- How the teachers receive feedback regarding the progress of the implementation of the initiative was clearly explained and offered.

- When the teachers receive feedback regarding the progress of the implementation of the initiative was clearly explained and offered.

How well did you establish and how often did you clarify the method for continued support of implementation by offering the following support?

- How the teachers identify when they are succeeding and when they are struggling was clearly explained and offered.

- The supports teachers receive if they are struggling were clearly explained and offered.

- How the teachers will have a say in determining their needs was clearly explained and offered.

How well and how often did you share the information with the staff by offering the following support?

- The information was explained, defined, and shared in as many distinct ways as possible.

Table 3.10: Narrative Reflection on the Implementation of the Actions of Instructional Leadership in Assessment

Reflect on the Implementation of the Actions of Instructional Leadership in Assessment

All support and learning is driven by regular assessment that guides decision-making.

To what degree did you confirm the success criteria for the initiative?

- The success criteria of the initiative were clearly explained and defined.

5	4	3	2	1
always		sometimes		never

- How the teachers know that they have implemented the initiative at a high level was clearly explained and defined.

5	4	3	2	1
always		sometimes		never

To what degree did you clarify the method for monitoring the implementation of the initiative?

- How the teachers receive feedback regarding the progress of the implementation of the initiative was clearly explained and offered.

5	4	3	2	1
always		sometimes		never

- When the teachers receive feedback regarding the progress of the implementation of the initiative was clearly explained and offered.

5	4	3	2	1
always		sometimes		never

To what degree did you clarify the method for continued support of implementation?

- How the teachers identify when they are succeeding and when they are struggling was clearly explained and offered.

5	4	3	2	1
always		sometimes		never

- The supports teachers receive if they are struggling were clearly explained and offered.

5	4	3	2	1
always		sometimes		never

- How the teachers will have a say in determining their needs was clearly explained and offered.

5	4	3	2	1
always		sometimes		never

To what degree did you share the information with the staff?

- The information was explained, defined, and shared in as many distinct ways as possible.

5	4	3	2	1
always		sometimes		never

Table 3.11: Evaluative Reflection on the Implementation of the Actions of Instructional Leadership in Assessment

4 CLIMATE
The Value of a Professional Learning Environment

When you hear the word *climate*, what do you think of? We bet you think of the classroom environment or the school environment. We know that a classroom environment should be one that encourages, engages, and excites the students to want to enter and be ready to learn. We know that the school environment should be one that encourages, engages, and excites the student body to have pride in their school because they feel it is the best around. And, we know that principals need to attend to both environments.

However, that is not the type of climate we are talking about when we focus on instructional leadership. The climate we are talking about is the climate needed to support the implementation of an initiative that will increase student achievement. This climate is needed to support those who are implementing an initiative that ultimately increases student achievement. It is a climate to support adults in owning their own learning. Your task is to build an environment that encourages, engages, and excites the adults to implement the initiative at the highest level possible. When you do this, you will ensure that **all support and learning is driven by a positive climate**.

The Driving Force in Climate

A principal who is utilizing instructional leadership is a principal who treats teachers as learners and offers them all of the supports we would offer a student in the classroom. Teachers need to be part of a community that invites them to learn. So, it is up to the principal to facilitate the invitational climate.

Purkey and Stanley (1991) describe this as a model of invitational learning and base it on four propositions:

1. Trust, in that we need to convince not coerce others to engage in what we would like them to consider worthwhile activities;

2. Respect, in that we adopt caring and appropriate behaviors when treating others;

3. Optimism, in seeking the untapped potential and uniqueness in others;

4. Intentionality, in which we create programs by people designed to invite learning.

One of the ways you build this type of environment is to make sure all stakeholders are clear on all expectations. You do this when you pay attention to the curriculum of the initiative. In fact, you probably recognize that having the teachers be part of this decision-making is one step in building a positive climate.

Another way you build this environment is by supporting your teachers with a variety of professional learning opportunities. You pay attention to this when you determine the instruction of the initiative. In addition, you recognize that giving teachers a say in the type of support they want also builds a positive climate.

> The climate we are talking about is the climate needed to support the implementation of an initiative that will increase student achievement . . . Your task is to build an environment that encourages, engages, and excites the adults to implement the initiative at the highest level possible.

Ensuring that the monitoring of the initiative is driven by the need for improvement and not the need for compliance is another way to build this type of environment. You focus on this when you address the assessment of the initiative. You also know that listening to the teachers and their notions of success, areas of growth, and their own next steps builds a positive climate.

Thus, you have been building a positive climate when you address the supports in curriculum, instruction, and assessment. You have been building a positive climate when you clearly communicate all expectations for each stakeholder. The initiative you have selected to increase student achievement is at such a level that it cannot be implemented piecemeal, individually, or on an ad hoc basis. It must be implemented collectively. As Deal and Peterson (1999) express it,

> While policymakers and reformers are pressing for new structures and more rational assessments, it is important to remember that these changes cannot be successful without cultural support. *School cultures, in short, are key to school achievement and student learning.* (p. xii)

Thus, the purpose of climate is to build a respectful, cooperative, and collaborative environment that allows for the success of the initiative.

Positive school climate is built on developing ownership, and developing ownership begins when the principal looks at climate from the point of view of those implementing the initiative. What is clear is that when there is a climate that promotes ownership and teachers working together, the teachers themselves benefit. Research bears this out:

> The research on teacher collaboration—everywhere—is unequivocal. Collaborating with colleagues—and the culture of trust and knowledge sharing that collaboration produces—has been linked to increased teacher effectiveness, improved student test-score gains (Kraft & Papay, 2014), and teacher willingness to adopt new innovations (Granovetter & Soong, 1983). (Burns & Lawrie, 2016, p. 2)

Research also bears out that when the teachers benefit, the students benefit.

> When teachers and schools engage in high-quality collaboration, it leads to better achievement gains in math and reading for students. In addition, teachers improve at greater rates when they work in schools with better collaboration quality (Ronfeldt et al., 2015). (Vega, 2015, p. 5)

The role of the teacher in this learning climate is key. Their role is to actively pursue their own learning while respectfully, cooperatively, and collaboratively helping others actively pursue their learning. This is a positive climate that builds ownership.

What can a principal do to move a teacher toward owning their learning regarding their role in the learning climate? Remember, ownership is best defined as a mindset. Teachers who know they have the authority, the capacity, and the responsibility to own how they are learning during this process have an ownership mindset. Thus, to support a teacher to strengthen this mindset, the principal must delegate the authority, build the capacity, and give the responsibility to each and every teacher involved in the implementation.

The Imperatives for Ownership of Climate

To develop ownership, several things are imperative. It is imperative for all stakeholders—principals, assistant principals, instructional coaches, and teachers—to know and be able to articulate their role in the successful implementation of the initiative. It is imperative for all stakeholders to know that the staff as a whole is more effective than any one individual. It is imperative that all stakeholders articulate their role in building a respectful, cooperative, and collaborative school climate. It is imperative that they understand the value of recognizing and promoting each other. It is imperative for them to honor risk-taking and understand how struggling is a crucial aspect of the learning process—for them and their colleagues. It is imperative that they support each other in the learning process and the implementation of the initiative. It is imperative that each stakeholder values cooperative and collaborative work as a support to the successful implementation of the initiative.

Table 4.1 provides some helpful indicators that reveal when stakeholders are taking ownership of their learning.

If all stakeholders are able to articulate the points in this chart effectively, they understand what is needed to build a respectful, cooperative, and collaborative

> It is imperative for all stakeholders to know that the staff as a whole is more effective than any one individual. It is imperative that all stakeholders articulate their role in building a respectful, cooperative, and collaborative school climate. It is imperative that they understand the value of recognizing and promoting each other.

> ## How Do Stakeholders Demonstrate Ownership of Climate?
>
> Each and every stakeholder is able to articulate:
> - The goals of the initiative
> - The success criteria of the initiative
> - The role of the teacher in the implementation of the initiative
> - The role of the principal in the implementation of the initiative
> - The role of the coach in the implementation of the initiative
> - The value of a cooperative environment to encourage risk-taking
> - The value of a collaborative environment to strengthen implementation
> - The role of each stakeholder in a cooperative and collaborative environment

Table 4.1: Indicators of Ownership of Climate

school climate. This understanding also builds an interdependence that will allow the implementation of the initiative to become less stressful for any one individual.

> The positive interdependence that binds group members together is posited to result in feelings of responsibility for (a) completing one's share of the work and (b) facilitating the work of other group members. (Johnson & Johnson, 2009, p. 368)

All of this leads to strengthening schoolwide ownership.

Move Beyond Doing and Understanding to Owning Climate

What does ownership look like in practice? What does it sound like when a teacher owns their part in the climate of the initiative? What is the difference between a teacher who is simply *doing* the work or *understanding* the initiative and one who is *owning* their role in the initiative?

A teacher is *doing* when they can state their duties.

A teacher is *understanding* when they can explain the value and purpose of their role and the roles of other stakeholders.

A teacher is *owning* their role in the initiative when they can articulate the value and purpose of their role in the initiative; the value and purpose of the role of other stakeholders in the initiative; the value and purpose of creating a respectful, cooperative, and collaborative environment; the value and purpose of supporting others to take risks; and the value and purpose of taking risks during implementation.

The tables that follow present some examples of what this looks like and sounds like on a continuum of doing–understanding–owning in a variety of initiatives, particularly when we ask the question, "What is your role in the initiative?"

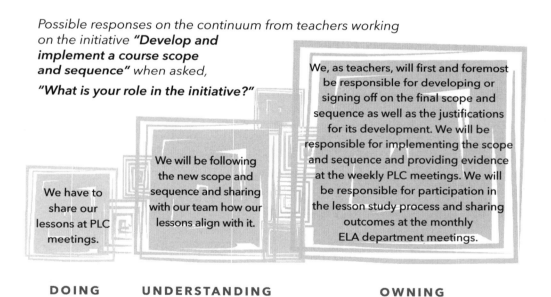

Possible responses on the continuum from teachers working on the initiative **"Develop and implement a course scope and sequence"** when asked,

"What is your role in the initiative?"

We have to share our lessons at PLC meetings.

We will be following the new scope and sequence and sharing with our team how our lessons align with it.

We, as teachers, will first and foremost be responsible for developing or signing off on the final scope and sequence as well as the justifications for its development. We will be responsible for implementing the scope and sequence and providing evidence at the weekly PLC meetings. We will be responsible for participation in the lesson study process and sharing outcomes at the monthly ELA department meetings.

DOING   UNDERSTANDING   OWNING

Table 4.2: Ownership Continuum of Climate When Developing and Implementing a Course Scope and Sequence

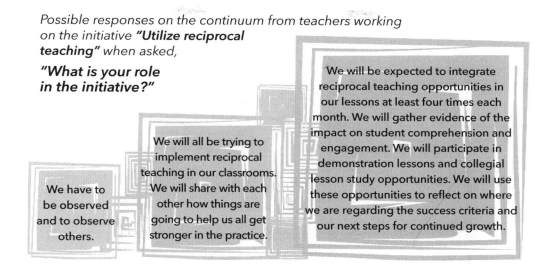

Possible responses on the continuum from teachers working on the initiative **"Utilize reciprocal teaching"** *when asked,*

"What is your role in the initiative?"

We have to be observed and to observe others.

We will all be trying to implement reciprocal teaching in our classrooms. We will share with each other how things are going to help us all get stronger in the practice.

We will be expected to integrate reciprocal teaching opportunities in our lessons at least four times each month. We will gather evidence of the impact on student comprehension and engagement. We will participate in demonstration lessons and collegial lesson study opportunities. We will use these opportunities to reflect on where we are regarding the success criteria and our next steps for continued growth.

DOING   **UNDERSTANDING**   **OWNING**

Table 4.3: Ownership Continuum of Climate When Utilizing a Specific Instructional Strategy, Reciprocal Teaching

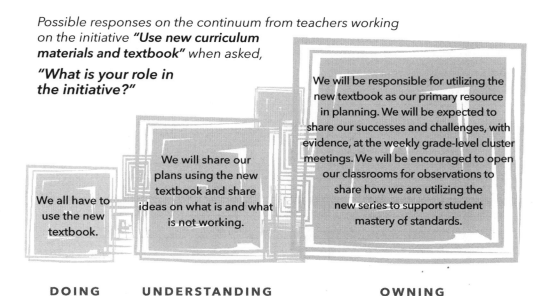

Possible responses on the continuum from teachers working on the initiative **"Use new curriculum materials and textbook"** *when asked,*

"What is your role in the initiative?"

We all have to use the new textbook.

We will share our plans using the new textbook and share ideas on what is and what is not working.

We will be responsible for utilizing the new textbook as our primary resource in planning. We will be expected to share our successes and challenges, with evidence, at the weekly grade-level cluster meetings. We will be encouraged to open our classrooms for observations to share how we are utilizing the new series to support student mastery of standards.

DOING   **UNDERSTANDING**   **OWNING**

Table 4.4: Ownership Continuum of Climate When Using New Curriculum Materials and Textbook

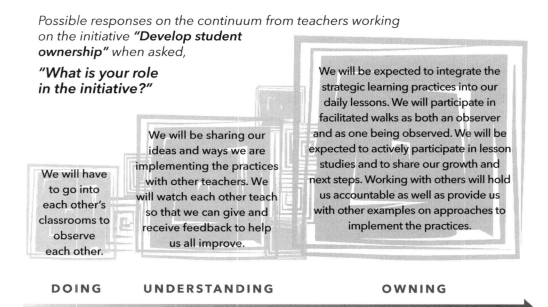

Possible responses on the continuum from teachers working on the initiative *"Develop student ownership"* when asked,

"What is your role in the initiative?"

We will have to go into each other's classrooms to observe each other.

We will be sharing our ideas and ways we are implementing the practices with other teachers. We will watch each other teach so that we can give and receive feedback to help us all improve.

We will be expected to integrate the strategic learning practices into our daily lessons. We will participate in facilitated walks as both an observer and as one being observed. We will be expected to actively participate in lesson studies and to share our growth and next steps. Working with others will hold us accountable as well as provide us with other examples on approaches to implement the practices.

DOING   UNDERSTANDING   OWNING

Table 4.5: Ownership Continuum of Climate When Developing Student Ownership

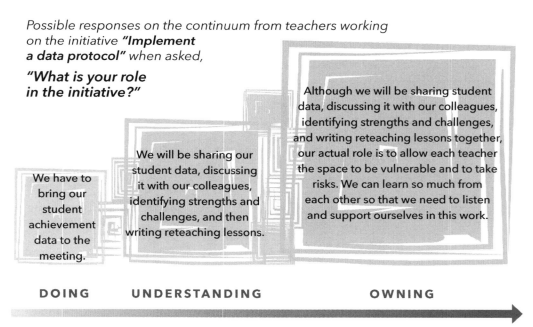

Possible responses on the continuum from teachers working on the initiative *"Implement a data protocol"* when asked,

"What is your role in the initiative?"

We have to bring our student achievement data to the meeting.

We will be sharing our student data, discussing it with our colleagues, identifying strengths and challenges, and then writing reteaching lessons.

Although we will be sharing student data, discussing it with our colleagues, identifying strengths and challenges, and writing reteaching lessons together, our actual role is to allow each teacher the space to be vulnerable and to take risks. We can learn so much from each other so that we need to listen and support ourselves in this work.

DOING   UNDERSTANDING   OWNING

Table 4.6: Ownership Continuum of Climate When Implementing a Data Protocol

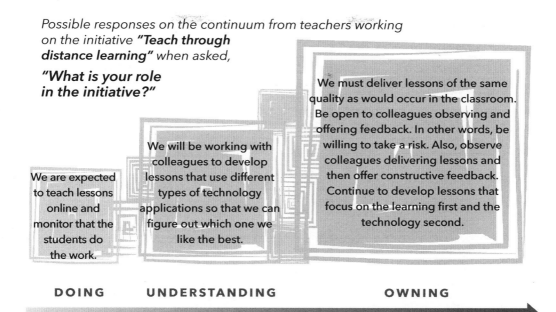

*Possible responses on the continuum from teachers working on the initiative **"Teach through distance learning"** when asked,*

"What is your role in the initiative?"

We are expected to teach lessons online and monitor that the students do the work.

We will be working with colleagues to develop lessons that use different types of technology applications so that we can figure out which one we like the best.

We must deliver lessons of the same quality as would occur in the classroom. Be open to colleagues observing and offering feedback. In other words, be willing to take a risk. Also, observe colleagues delivering lessons and then offer constructive feedback. Continue to develop lessons that focus on the learning first and the technology second.

DOING   UNDERSTANDING   OWNING

Table 4.7: Ownership Continuum of Climate When Teaching through Distance Learning

The Practices That Drive Instructional Leadership in Climate

Although there are hundreds of strategies a principal could use during implementation, we will focus on the three practices in climate that research shows increase the opportunities for learning—by increasing the opportunities for ownership. The following three strategic learning practices are what your adult learners need in order to learn.

- **Strategic Learning Practice, Climate 1:** Adults are supported by a respectful environment that recognizes and promotes professional behavior.

- **Strategic Learning Practice, Climate 2:** Adults are supported by a cooperative environment that encourages risk-taking.

- **Strategic Learning Practice, Climate3:** Adults are supported by a collaborative environment that enhances individual productivity.

Let's begin by defining each aspect of the three practices.

Strategic Learning Practice, Climate 1: Adults are supported by a **respectful** environment that **recognizes** and **promotes professional behaviors**.

Respectful is the cornerstone attribute of an effective and efficient school. This means that leadership and teachers honor and accept each other as professionals and individuals with specific learning strengths and needs.

Recognizes is the intentional acknowledgment of professional behaviors, specific and public.

Promotes is the intentional acknowledgment of professional behaviors to nurture and advance the learning.

Professional behaviors include those actions that support learning—such as perseverance, effort, resourcefulness, self-management, reflection, precision, and active participation—and lead to increased learner ownership.

Strategic Learning Practice, Climate 2: Adults are supported by a **cooperative** environment that **encourages risk-taking**.

Cooperative describes the mutual assistance of individuals as they join together to achieve a common learning outcome. It allows for collegial support toward success in the initiative outcome.

Encourages means to give support, confidence, and hope to the learner and their efforts.

Risk-taking is the act of taking a chance, knowing failure may occur on the first attempt, in order to achieve an expectation that presents a challenge to the learner. Risk-takers know that true learning is about change and that change takes effort; they also willingly accept the challenge of struggle.

Strategic Learning Practice, Climate 3: Adults are supported by a **collaborative** environment that **enhances individual productivity**.

Collaborative comes from the Latin word *laborare*, which means *to work*. When we co-labor, we work together. In other words, teachers are working alongside other teachers to achieve or produce something of higher quality than they could on their own.

Enhances is to intensify, increase, or further improve the quality of the learning.

Individual productivity describes the effectiveness of the effort of individuals as they are learning. Via a collaborative approach, individual learning is increased.

Thus, all support and learning must be driven by a positive climate because:

1. When teachers are supported by a respectful environment that recognizes and promotes professional behavior, they have a better chance to be successful.

2. When teachers are supported by a cooperative environment that encourages risk-taking, they have a better chance to be successful.

3. When teachers are supported by a collaborative environment that enhances individual productivity, they have a better chance to be successful.

These practices form the foundation of the clear and consistent actions the principal must take to support their teachers' ownership of their learning to ensure successful implementation of the initiative.

How does a principal do this? They must model the thinking behind the ownership and explicitly address the skills of ownership. This takes planning. In order for all stakeholders to answer these questions—"What is the teachers' role in the implementation of the initiative?" "How will the teachers support each other in the implementation of the initiative?" and "How will the teachers be supported to take risks in the implementation of the initiative?"—principals must be strategic in the actions they use to support staff.

In other words, these three strategic learning practices translate into the four actions of instructional leadership in climate:

▸ Identify the role of each stakeholder in the implementation of the initiative.

▸ Foster cooperation among and between stakeholders.

▸ Establish a plan for collaboration.

▸ ***Share this information with the staff.***

To lead the actions of climate, the principal must ensure that all stakeholders understand that a positive school environment is crucial if teachers are to take risks in their learning. A positive climate is one that is built on respect, cooperation, and collaboration. The more positive the climate, the more readily that teachers encourage and welcome feedback from the principal and their colleagues, that teachers work together to enhance and deepen one another's learning, and that teachers support one another to take risks in their learning. Use your faculty and staff to develop the actions that build a respectful, cooperative, and collaborative climate. Your task is to lead these actions.

> . . . we need leaders who create a culture of growth; know how to engage the hearts and minds of everyone; and focus their collective intelligence, talent, commitment to shaping a new path. They recognize that what pulls people in is meaningful work in collaboration with others. They *use the group to change the group* by building deep collaborative work horizontally and vertically across their organizations. (Fullan & Quinn, 2016, p. 47)

In addition, don't forget, you must continuously, purposefully, and intentionally share assessment information with the staff. This is the notion of conceptual redundancy. If you think your teachers need to hear the information again, you're right and they do. If you think your staff does not need to hear the information again, you're wrong because they do.

Questions to Guide Implementing the Actions of Instructional Leadership in Climate

All support and learning is driven by a positive climate.

Use these planning questions to focus your support.

Identify the role of each stakeholder in the implementation of the initiative.

❑ What is the role of the teacher in the implementation of the initiative?

❑ What is the role of the principal in the implementation of the initiative?

❑ What is the role of the coach in the implementation of the initiative?

Foster cooperation among and between stakeholders.

❑ How will the teachers be supported and encouraged to take risks in the implementation of the initiative?

Establish a plan for collaboration.

❑ What is the purpose and value of collaborative support?

❑ What is the role of each teacher in a collaborative opportunity?

❑ When will teachers work together to support each other in the implementation of the initiative?

Share this information with the staff.

❑ How will this information be shared in as many distinct ways as possible?

Table 4.8: Questions to Guide Implementing the Actions of Instructional Leadership in Climate

An Example of Teacher Ownership in Climate

WHERE: An elementary school led by Principal Balsamo

WHAT: The initiative is the implementation of a data analysis protocol.

WHO: The second-grade team at a K–5 school

Let's hear what these teachers had to say about the initiative as they were asked these questions regarding climate:

> ▶ *What is the teachers' role in the implementation of the initiative?*
>
> ▶ *How will the teachers support each other in the implementation of the initiative?*
>
> ▶ *How will the teachers be supported to take risks in the implementation of the initiative?*

First, we asked, *"What is the initiative you are implementing?"*

TEACHER 1:   "We are implementing a data analysis protocol. Our school has recently seen a decline in math scores. We knew we couldn't wait until we gave the summative assessments to determine what our students hadn't learned. We would have to frequently look at data to see whether or not they are progressing."

TEACHER 2:   "We also knew we didn't want to just look at data. We needed a process that would allow us not just to analyze the student data but to take a close look at the instructional decisions we made along the way. And how those decisions impacted student learning."

Then, *"How will you all support each other in the implementation of your data analysis protocol?"*

TEACHER 3:   "We have scheduled PLC time each week for our protocol. This is the time for us to bring all of our collective information and knowledge to the table. This can't be about your students or my students. This can't be about your class or my class. This has to be about our students. This has to be about our school."

TEACHER 2:   "When Mrs. Balsamo introduced this initiative to us, she was clear that this was about us all working together to lift our students' achievement. If we want all of our students to move on and be successful in math, then it couldn't be that change just occurs in one room. We need to work together and share our efforts."

TEACHER 1:   "So during our PLCs, we analyze the data together. We identify areas of strength and challenges. If one teacher is finding greater success with a skill, then we need to determine what occurred so we can all replicate it. If we are finding a lack of success across the board, we need to work together to find other approaches that will support our students. We have also established times that we can observe a teacher who is finding success as they teach a particular skill to see and discuss what they are doing that is supporting student learning."

TEACHER 4:   "At some grade levels, we are also grouping across the classrooms. If we have a group of students from different rooms that need reteaching or even acceleration, we regroup and provide that differentiation. It has made it easier than trying to differentiate it all in our classroom alone."

We responded, *"It sounds like teachers have to be open to sharing and trying new things. How will the teachers be supported to take risks in the implementation of the initiative?"*

TEACHER 2:   "Yes, for many of us, this took us out of our comfort zone. We have been used to just focusing on what we do in our room. We didn't necessarily share our successes and challenges with each other."

TEACHER 3:   "The truth is that our math scores aren't great. We want to change this. We know that lasting change happens when we support each other—when we are not only accountable to ourselves but to each other. And that will require we take some risks, expose our areas of need, share our successes, and work together."

TEACHER 4:   "Mrs. Balsamo has told us over and over that this will take time. But our data analysis protocol will allow us to track our progress along the way. It will show where our risks are paying off for student learning. Having the message of all of us being in this together for student learning makes risk-taking easier."

These answers show clarity of focus that demonstrates these teachers are on their way to owning their learning when it comes to this initiative. But, how did they get here? How did Principal Balsamo implement the actions of instructional leadership in climate?

An Example of Instructional Leadership in Climate

Principal Balsamo explained that she knew her task was to determine and lead these actions:

▸ Identify the role of each stakeholder in the implementation of the initiative.

▸ Foster cooperation among and between stakeholders.

▸ Establish a plan for collaboration.

▸ Share this information with the staff.

She began the process by answering the questions from the planning chart on page 107.

▸ *What is the role of the teacher in the implementation of the initiative?*

▸ *What is the role of the principal in the implementation of the initiative?*

▸ *What is the role of the coach in the implementation of the initiative?*

PRINCIPAL BALSAMO: "We have seen a collective decrease in our students' math scores. We knew that some of this had to do with our new standards and new assessments. Many of our teachers were not adapting to the new expectations but were instead doing what they had always done in math instruction. This was not serving our students well at all. But me just telling the teachers that we needed to change wasn't going to do it. We had to really understand what our students were and were not grasping in math. We needed a process to analyze data and instruction and make changes based on it."

"I knew that the teachers had the most critical role in this initiative. They were the ones that we were asking to take risks, share their successes and challenges with each other, and make changes. We needed a process that would hold them accountable to themselves and each other. By looking at the data collectively and making sure our conversations were about student learning and not about teachers, we have found greater participation and cooperation than ever before."

"But I knew that even though they have the most crucial role, this work could not rest on their shoulders alone. They would need support from me and from our math coach. My most important role is to communicate, communicate, communicate. I have to be certain every teacher understands the goals and success criteria of the initiative, that they understand the plan we have in place to support them as they implement it, and that we are all accountable for the success of it. My second most important role is to be available for the teachers and to have strong conversations with them. As I meet with grade levels or individuals, I make sure I am asking the right questions and honoring the strong decisions they are making, the risks they are taking, and how they are supporting each other. We make sure we celebrate our successes along the way."

"Our math coach also has an important role. He attends each PLC meeting. He is our school expert on the standards, the assessment expectations, and a variety of instructional resources and strategies. When teachers hit roadblocks with skills, his role is to help them understand the skill better and to find approaches they can try to support learning. He knows which teachers are showing success and sets up visits to have them be observed. He also does demonstration lessons so teachers can see the new strategies in action."

Once the roles had been determined, Principal Balsamo then had to determine the following:

> ▶ *How will the teachers be supported and encouraged to take risks in the implementation of the initiative?*

PRINCIPAL BALSAMO: "The best way I have learned to support others to take risks is to take them myself. I am very vocal with the teachers about the decisions I make. I let them know when I am taking a smart risk and why. I let them know when my risks pay off and when I fail miserably. But I always share with them what I learned from each risk—the successful and unsuccessful ones. Modeling is the best way I can support and encourage them to take risks. But it doesn't stop with modeling. I also need them to know that risk-taking is safe and encouraged at this school. We publicly celebrate how we get out of our comfort zone for our students' learning. I know that these acknowledgments need to be real, relevant, and public. The more the teachers see each other taking risks and that all that comes from it is learning, not judgment or evaluation, the more they are willing to take risks and support each other."

Principal Balsamo knew that she could not do all of the work alone. She needed the teachers to work as a team. She then determined:

> ▶ *What is the purpose and value of collaborative support?*
>
> ▶ *What is the role of each teacher in a collaborative opportunity?*
>
> ▶ *When will teachers work together to support each other in the implementation of the initiative?*

PRINCIPAL BALSAMO: "At a leadership session I attended, the presenter talked about a book called *Change or Die*. It sounded quite gruesome. But the speaker told us the book was about how sustainable change happens. And it happens when individuals are accountable to themselves and others. He gave a quick example of going to the gym. It is easy for us to tell ourselves we will change and go there regularly. It is just as easy to not go. But if your friend is meeting you at the gym, you're not going to not meet them. I shared this with my teachers and let them know that we needed to be a group that worked together for our common goals. That we couldn't be a school of 'I's but needed to be a 'We.'"

"But this is easy to espouse. The harder part is to get teachers, especially those who are used to just staying in their classroom and closing the door, to believe in and value this. This comes from making certain the teachers are very clear on their role in collaboration. Some of the teachers are willing participants. But for others, they need a defined role and expectation until it becomes just what we do."

"For our weekly PLCs, each teacher must bring their agreed-upon formative data for the skills taught that week. They first share the data and look for patterns and trends across the classrooms. They then identify areas of success and areas of challenge. Whether it was successful or not, the teachers must share their instructional approach and why they chose that approach. These conversations were a bit stilted when we began. But it has become the way we talk about data and learning now. They all have a role in sharing."

"Beyond the weekly PLCs, teachers can request time to observe others and discuss. We also have some grade levels that have set up a time each week that they group students across the classrooms to differentiate based on their data analysis. I have been so impressed with the team approach they have taken."

To ensure that her message was clearly articulated and understood, Principal Balsamo had to determine:

> ▸ *How will the information be shared in as many distinct ways as possible?*

PRINCIPAL BALSAMO: "There were parts of the initiative that I shared with the staff and parts that I needed them to determine. Even when I shared a part—for example, the goal and success criteria of the data analysis protocol—I made certain they had time to discuss it and then articulate it in their own words.

An example of the part I needed them to determine was what their role would be in a PLC meeting. We outlined the purpose and value of the meetings. I then had the teachers come up with what would be their role, what was expected of each individual and what was expected of the group."

"We also use each staff meeting as a time to remind ourselves about our initiative and then to check in on our progress. I have found that this level of consistent communication and articulation has helped us become what we wanted. A school of 'we' rather than a school of individual 'I's."

How Other Administrators Utilize Instructional Leadership in Climate

INITIATIVE: Implementing a writing initiative

ADMINISTRATOR: Assistant principal of a high school

"We are implementing a schoolwide writing initiative. It is requiring all of us to plan and work together toward our determined outcomes to improve student learning by increasing their writing skills and ability to communicate their learning daily. I knew this was going to be a huge lift for us as a school. Our teachers are used to working and planning in departments, but not as an entire faculty. But our students don't work in departments, so why do we? I have a quote by Robert Eaker pinned up in my office. It says, "The traditional school often functions as a collection of independent contractors united by a common parking lot." Although the quote can be seen as humorous, it is unfortunately often true. We have done a lot of work to make certain this wasn't true in our school. But until this initiative, our school was a collection of department contractors. Now that we have laid the foundation of cooperation and collaboration in departments, we are utilizing this initiative as our opportunity to expand that to the entire staff. I know we will hit a few barriers, but we are moving in the right direction."

INITIATIVE: Developing student ownership

ADMINISTRATOR: Principal at K–8 school

"We are implementing an initiative to develop student ownership. We have developed a comprehensive plan for the year to support our teachers. A critical part of our plan is the lesson study process. After training on the process, teachers are paired up. They share with each other where they are in the implementation, what support they are currently focusing on, and the decisions they made for that day's lesson. They then observe each other, have a debrief conversation to discuss the impact they are seeing on student ownership, to clarify their decisions, and to push each other's thinking. It is a really powerful process. But, it can also be a logistical nightmare with scheduling and determining pairings. I decided that it was important that the teachers were empowered to own this process. After we established what must occur, the desired outcomes, how this process supported the initiative goals, and the value of collaboration, I handed it off to the teachers. They worked together to determine who, when, and how they would organize their lesson studies. My role was to make certain that coverage was in place as needed and to monitor how the process was supporting us to meet our goals. Now, I did step in and assign some teachers with a partner. But these are teachers that have specific needs, and I have been communicating with them along the way on their individual plan. Allowing the teachers to own this process has been powerful. We have greater buy-in and I saved a lot of time planning the details."

INITIATIVE: Using online social science textbooks

ADMINISTRATOR: Assistant principal of a high school

"We recently moved from print textbooks for our social science classes to an online program. We knew this initiative meant a lot of changes. Teachers had to learn the new online program and all of its capabilities, they had to understand the technology, and in some situations, they had to shift how they taught. We knew it was important that we valued innovations and risk-taking from our teachers. They had to know from the onset that these new materials would not drive their decision-making as teachers. They would continue to have the standards and student learning as the driver of their decisions. We gave them the freedom to try a variety of approaches using online-only resources. We just asked them to share with each other what they tried, what were the successes, what were the challenges, and what were their next steps. Giving them the freedom to make these decisions and risks could only have happened because of the climate of professionalism we had been fostering for years. Our teachers are getting more confident each day in navigating and implementing the online materials. They are learning from each other, and our students' learning has continued."

What Teachers Say About Instructional Leadership in Climate

INITIATIVE: Teaching through distance learning

TEACHER: Third-grade teacher

"We are implementing a learning management system to allow for distance learning. I am not comfortable with technology. Our principal is not either. Our principal decided that he needed to learn along with us. He has set up our staff as his classroom. He has created all of the communication and the plan for our initiative in this classroom. He even did some online lessons on the LMS with us so we could see the experience from the student perspective. But more importantly, he has shared with us every frustration and success he has had along the way. Seeing him willing to learn and take risks, and honestly fail at times, has made it easier for me to do the same. It reminds me that we are all learners and that we are in this together."

INITIATIVE: Implementing an English language arts scope and sequence and integrated units

TEACHER: Eighth-grade teacher

"Our ELA department is developing a standards-based scope and sequence with integrated units that lead to a piece of writing. This initiative requires us to analyze our standards, determine a scope and sequence for the year, develop strong writing prompts, identify curriculum resources, and sequence out the units. In the past, this type of work would fall on the shoulders of a few teachers. That usually meant some had ownership of the work and really embraced it. Others would pick and choose what they liked. And some disregarded it completely. Our principal has reminded us that this is about all of our students' learning. It can't happen in some places and not others. We decided that we all had to be a part of the development. But that can lead to too many cooks in the kitchen. So, as a team, we scoped out the work. We got to choose where we thought we could offer the most. We determined the roles and responsibilities of each person and the outcomes for each product. We discussed the interdependencies of each part and how they all lead to a strong final outcome. Having this clarity and understanding of our roles and expectations is allowing us to all work together. I am excited to see how it is coming along and I can't wait to see the final product."

Climate Reflection

How well do you develop your staff to own their role in learning with regard to the initiative?

In this chapter, we have shown you what ownership looks like in practice. We have shown you what it sounds like when teachers own their part in climate. And we have given examples of how principals have utilized the actions of instructional leadership in order to better support the successful implementation of the selected initiative.

We have also explained the differences between teachers who are simply *doing* or *understanding* climate and those who are *owning* their role in learning and implementing.

Remember, we said that a teacher is *doing* when they can state their duties.

Remember, we said that a teacher is *understanding* when they can explain the value and purpose of their role and the roles of other stakeholders.

Remember, we said a teacher is *owning* their role in the initiative when they can articulate the value and purpose of their role in the initiative; the value and purpose of the role of other stakeholders in the initiative; the value and purpose of creating a respectful, cooperative, and collaborative environment; the value and purpose of supporting others to take risks; and the value and purpose of taking risks during implementation.

Think of your teachers and staff. When you ask them these questions, what do they say?

"What is the teachers' role in the implementation of the initiative?"

"How will the teachers support each other in the implementation of the initiative?"

"How will the teachers be supported to take risks in the implementation of the initiative?"

Listen to their answers. Where do they fall on the doing–understanding–owning continuum? Think about the supports they need from you to develop ownership. How often and to what degree do you offer these supports? In other words, what impact do you have on leading the initiative and developing ownership?

John Hattie's research (2012) revealed that "Such passion for evaluating impact is the single most critical lever for instructional excellence—accompanied by understanding this impact and doing something in light of the evidence and understanding (p. viii).

What follows are reflection activities that will help you determine your impact on ownership—both areas of strength and areas of growth. These activities will help you understand how you utilize the actions of instructional leadership from the point of view of who you are leading—the teachers and your staff.

> To lead the actions of climate, the principal must ensure that all stakeholders understand that a positive school environment is crucial if teachers are to take risks in their learning. A positive climate is one that is built on respect, cooperation, and collaboration.

Remember that to develop ownership, all support and learning must be driven by a clearly defined initiative with measurable and achievable outcomes.

Also, remember that your actions are key to the development of ownership and the successful implementation of the initiative.

Reflect on the Implementation of the Actions of Instructional Leadership in Climate

All support and learning is driven by a positive climate.

How well and how often did you identify the role of each stakeholder in the implementation of the initiative by offering the following supports?

- The role of the teachers in the implementation of the initiative was clearly explained and defined.

- The role of the principal in the implementation of the initiative was clearly explained and defined.

- The role of the coach in the implementation of the initiative was clearly explained and defined.

How well and how often did you foster cooperation among and between stakeholders by offering the following support?

- How the teachers are supported and encouraged to take risks in the implementation of the initiative was clearly explained and offered.

How well did you establish and how often did you clarify the plan for collaboration by offering the following support?

- The purpose and value of collaborative support was clearly explained and defined.

- The role of each teacher in a collaborative opportunity was clearly explained and defined.

- When the teachers work together to support each other in the implementation of the initiative was clearly explained and offered.

How well and how often did you share the information with the staff by offering the following support?

- The information was explained, defined, and shared in as many distinct ways as possible.

Table 4.9: Narrative Reflection on the Implementation of the Actions of Instructional Leadership in Climate

Reflect on the Implementation of the Actions of Instructional Leadership in Climate

All support and learning is driven by a positive climate.

To what degree did you identify the role of each stakeholder in the implementation of the initiative?

- The role of the teachers in the implementation of the initiative was clearly explained and defined.

5	4	3	2	1
always		sometimes		never

- The role of the principal in the implementation of the initiative was clearly explained and defined.

5	4	3	2	1
always		sometimes		never

- The role of the coach in the implementation of the initiative was clearly explained and defined.

5	4	3	2	1
always		sometimes		never

To what degree did you foster cooperation among and between stakeholders?

- How the teachers are supported and encouraged to take risks in the implementation of the initiative was clearly explained and offered.

5	4	3	2	1
always		sometimes		never

To what degree did you clarify the plan for collaboration?

- The purpose and value of collaborative support was clearly explained and defined.

5	4	3	2	1
always		sometimes		never

- The role of each teacher in a collaborative opportunity was clearly explained and defined.

5	4	3	2	1
always		sometimes		never

- When the teachers work together to support each other in the implementation of the initiative was clearly explained and offered.

5	4	3	2	1
always		sometimes		never

To what degree did you share the information with the staff?

- The information was explained, defined, and shared in as many distinct ways as possible.

5	4	3	2	1
always		sometimes		never

Table 4.10: Evaluative Reflection on the Implementation of the Actions of Instructional Leadership in Climate

5 INSTRUCTIONAL LEADERSHIP IN ACTION

A Vignette About Implementing a Hybrid Learning Model

WHERE: A suburban elementary school in a diverse community

WHAT: The initiative is the implementation of a hybrid learning model that combines the effectiveness and socialization opportunities of direct teacher instruction in the classroom and the robust active learning opportunities offered through technology. The schedule for students will include working two days on campus, with alternate days working at home. Fridays will be used for intervention and reteaching support on-site, as needed.

WHO: Principal Lang, a principal for five years, three at his current location. He has already led initiatives in the implementation of an English language arts standards-based scope and sequence and a new mathematics curriculum and textbook. He also led a schoolwide initiative on developing a culture of student ownership.

HOW: Principal Lang utilized the actions of instructional leadership that take into account the strategic learning practices in curriculum, instruction, assessment, and climate.

What follows is our conversation with Principal Lang about his decision-making and implementation.

The Actions of Instructional Leadership in Curriculum

When speaking with Principal Lang about his new initiative, he explained that he knew that when it came to the curriculum of his initiative his task was to determine and lead these actions:

▸ Clarify the goals of the initiative.

▸ Integrate the goals of the initiative with other expectations.

▸ Decide the resources needed to implement the initiative.

▸ Share this information with the staff.

He began the process by answering the question from the planning chart on page 28.

▸ *What are the goals of the initiative?*

PRINCIPAL LANG: "We are implementing a hybrid learning model. This is allowing us to combine the effectiveness and socialization opportunities of the classroom with robust active learning that can be offered through technology. With a hybrid learning schedule that has fewer students in the classroom at a given time, our goal is to utilize both the classroom time and the technology time to increase interactions between students and teachers, between students and students, between students and the skills and content they are learning, and between students and outside resources."

Once that goal had been determined, Principal Lang then had to determine the following:

▸ *What is the purpose of the initiative?*

PRINCIPAL LANG: "Our ultimate goal is to increase student engagement and learning. Our teachers work hard. But the reality of a traditional classroom is that it can be difficult to maintain a level of high engagement, to find a pace that meets student's varying needs, and to offer the time for students to grapple with constructing meaning. And some of our teachers have fallen into the trap of 'getting through the lesson' rather than 'getting through to learning.'"

"Our student engagement has declined. Our academic data is showing a stagnation as well. Plus, we know we live in a digital age. Our students are comfortable with technology and crave the opportunity to work with it more. These factors, combined with health precautions, led us to a hybrid learning approach."

> ▸ *What, specifically, will the teacher be expected to implement?*
> ▸ *What, specifically, are the success criteria for the initiative?*

PRINCIPAL LANG: "Before we rolled out the initiative, we worked on the logistics of schedules. This took a great deal of time, but we pulled together a really smart team to tackle it. Our students are not all the same and we knew we could not have a one-size-fits-all solution. We approached it as an opportunity to enhance active learning possibilities using technology, rather than dividing up the schedule by types of delivery."

"We didn't want to define the model too specifically, such as for every lesson the students needed two hours of in-class, with one hour of virtual learning, and then one hour of completing the assignment on the computer. This wouldn't focus on the skills being learned. And opening this up gave us flexibility, so we weren't setting ourselves, or our students, up for failure had we tried to fit a square into a circle. Once the team had a schedule that took into consideration the students and the courses, I knew we had to bring this to the teachers and let them know what this meant to them—what was our expectation of them."

"We let the teachers know that the goals we had in place before had not changed. We are a school focused on developing student ownership. That work would continue. But now as we moved into a hybrid learning approach, we needed them to rethink planning. They would need to develop plans that took into consideration how they would utilize face-to-face instruction with synchronous and asynchronous instruction. We needed them to develop plans that had students actively engaged in the learning process, not just passively absorbing content."

"This meant that teachers needed to make decisions, and be able to justify these decisions, as to how they would use a hybrid learning environment to support their students to actively construct meaning and demonstrate understanding. We have looked at lesson plans in the past through the lens of the teacher. We also tended to look at them through a class or a learning session. We now are developing plans that are through the lens of our students, as well as plans that are chunked or built into units. We needed to identify what would be the final demonstration of learning for each unit, what would be the role of the learner throughout the unit, and how we would maximize the opportunities a hybrid learning environment offers to support students in engagement and achievement."

But Principal Lang knew that if he wanted real buy-in from his teachers, they would have to see the benefits to this work. He then had to determine:

> ▸ *How will the success of the initiative benefit the students?*

> ▸ *How will the success of the initiative benefit the teachers?*

PRINCIPAL LANG: "My teachers know their content well. This initiative had to leverage and honor that strength. But it was going to take work and it would force some folks to get out of their comfort zone. I knew they had to see value in this approach. It couldn't feel like something that was being 'done to them.'"

"We began by talking about what would be our ideal classroom. Not surprisingly, our teachers wanted fewer students and more time with the students. We then had them share why they would want this. What would be the benefit to the students and what would be the benefit to them? They had a lot of responses, but we were able to categorize them into four buckets. They felt this would allow them to know their students better, they could differentiate more easily, they could allow the students to take a more active role, and they could go deeper with the learning."

"We then examined some exemplar models of hybrid learning that had students engaged in meaningful and relevant learning. That fostered conceptual understanding and deep thinking. And that leveraged collaboration and communication. We discussed how these models would benefit our students and would benefit teachers regarding their ideal classrooms."

"Our final step was to then decide what would we want our school to look and sound like by the end of the year. We created our exemplar of highly engaged students that worked together to construct meaning and that leveraged the power of technology in a hybrid environment."

To ensure that his teachers did not feel overwhelmed, Principal Lang had to determine:

> ▸ *How does the initiative support the other work of the school?*

PRINCIPAL LANG: "As I mentioned earlier, we shared with the teachers that our work on developing student ownership would continue. But my saying it was not enough. I had to make certain my teachers saw how this work would only enhance what they have been doing. As we began to break down the details of the hybrid learning initiative, we aligned it to the practices we had in place."

"We have worked toward the goal of each and every student being able to articulate what they are learning and why they are learning it, how they will learn it, how they will know they are learning and what they will do if they struggle, and what their role is in a classroom of learners. These are questions you can ask any student, at any time, on our campus and you will get a fairly strong answer. We are working to strengthen those answers. Our next level on student ownership has been for students to articulate why knowing the answers to these questions is important to their learning. This work will not only continue but will be imperative to the success of this initiative. As we hand over more ownership of learning to our students in this hybrid environment, we must support them in understanding the value and necessity of knowing the learning goals and process so they can self-direct as needed."

To ensure that his teachers had sufficient resources and materials to successfully implement the initiative, Principal Lang had to determine:

> ▸ *What resources will the teacher need to effectively implement the initiative?*

PRINCIPAL LANG: "Our teachers would need several resources to be successful in this initiative. They would need models of exemplar hybrid learning units, access to colleagues for collegial planning, and technology tools and applications designed to maximize engagement.

"We had to do distance learning while schools were shut down because of COVID-19. Our staff is comfortable with the online platform and how to assign and receive work from students. They know how to deliver synchronous instruction and how to develop and push out asynchronous lessons."

"But during that time, we were mostly trying to recreate a classroom-type lesson in a distance learning environment. This is different. Our goal in this initiative is to increase student engagement and learning. So, our teachers need to know how to plan differently—through the lens of unit outcomes and student engagement. They need training on the potential of this and how to plan for it. They need dedicated time to collaborate with their colleagues and develop these plans. And finally, they need to know what technology tools they had available to use."

To ensure that his message was clearly articulated and understood, Principal Lang had to determine:

> *How will the information be shared in as many distinct ways as possible?*

PRINCIPAL LANG: "I learned a great deal when we communicated our initiative for the first time. No one got it. To put it in perspective, I remember teachers telling me that students seemed oblivious to their learning goals and plans."

"'But I told them!' they would say. 'Why are they saying they don't know?'"

"I realized that I actually did the same thing. I even said to them, 'But I told you! Why are you saying you didn't know?'"

"How embarrassing. Well, by grappling with this issue, we learned that just saying something once does not mean everyone understood or even heard it. We learned that, just like with students, the teachers needed to articulate it, in their own words, and more than once. So, I now do the same thing. As I share information, I have the teachers first talk to each other to put it in their own words and then share it with all of us. This allows us to know whether or not everyone has the same message. And if not, we can clarify as needed."

The Actions of Instructional Leadership in Instruction

After Principal Lang determined the curriculum decisions of this initiative, he then had to consider the instruction of the initiative. He knew his task was to determine and lead these actions:

> Establish a plan for professional learning opportunities.

> Clarify how the initiative will be supported and implemented.

> Schedule professional learning opportunities directly related to the initiative.

> Share this information with the staff.

He continued the process by answering the questions from the planning chart on page 55.

> ▸ *What supports will the teacher receive in order to achieve the goals of the initiative?*

PRINCIPAL LANG: "When I considered the outcome and the needs of the teachers, I knew our plan would require a range of supports. The team knew our teachers would need a deepened understanding of the potential of hybrid learning to increase student engagement and learning, the tools and time for effective planning and collaboration, training on the technology applications that would support our goals, and coaching by our experts."

"We outlined each of these areas and developed a year-long professional learning plan. Our plan included training opportunities, instruction and technology coaching, dedicated time for planning and PLC time for data analysis and reflection."

Once the variety of supports has been determined, Principal Lang then had to determine the following:

> ▸ *What is the expectation of the teacher for each provided support?*
>
> ▸ *How will teachers ask for and receive additional support?*
>
> ▸ *How will the teachers work together to implement the initiative?*
>
> ▸ *How will the teachers have opportunities to contribute ideas to the implementation plan?*

PRINCIPAL LANG: "The teachers and staff and I backward mapped from our determined end goal and established milestones for our initiative. We then aligned each support with those milestones so each teacher could see how they would be supported for continued growth. Our expectations of the teachers were also aligned with the supports."

"One thing that came up in our planning was the notion that teachers didn't know how to ask for support—they didn't want to take anyone's time. So, we developed a growth rubric that took the components of our ideal school goal and went from non-existent to fully existent. We asked teachers to determine where they thought they were in each category. After each training, coaching, or PLC opportunity, teachers were asked to explain how the support could help them grow, what their next steps in the implementation were, and what additional support they still needed. They felt much more comfortable asking for help when the process of how to ask for support was so clear cut."

But Principal Lang knew that he wanted to ensure focus on the initiative, so all of the supports must be related to the initiative. He wasn't willing to pull his teachers off the task. So, he then had to determine:

▸ *What is the timeline and plan for the initiative?*

▸ *When will the teachers receive support?*

▸ *What are the milestone expectations for each learner?*

PRINCIPAL LANG: "The team worked with department chairs on our professional learning plan. Once we were ready to share it with the staff, we knew we had to be very thoughtful in our delivery or it could be overwhelming."

"We began with the end in mind and reminded the teachers of where we wanted to get and how we had the entire year to get there. We also assured them that we would all monitor our progress along the way and adjust as needed. After that, we introduced the types of support that would be offered, from training, to coaching, to dedicated planning time, to PLCs for data analysis and reflection."

"We wanted them to see how it all connected and that it would be ongoing. As we looked at the plan in a calendar view, we overlaid the milestones and asked the teachers for feedback. Did they think there was enough support to meet each milestone or was there too much support in any area? We used their feedback to make some adjustments to the plan and once again reassured them that we would monitor and adjust along the way. Their success, and ultimately the student learning, was the goal."

To ensure that his message was clearly articulated and understood, Principal Lang had to determine:

▸ *How will the information be shared in as many distinct ways as possible?*

PRINCIPAL LANG: "I never began a meeting or conversation with a teacher without quickly reviewing the basics of the initiative. I used every opportunity to remind everyone of what we agreed we were implementing and why. This allowed teachers to hear it again and again and in a variety of situations. Because teachers are getting support in a variety of ways—initial professional development, working in small groups, or one-to-one—this allowed me, the admin team, or the instructional coaches to repeat the context for the initiative, the outcome of the initiative, or the expectations of the initiative, as many times as possible."

The Actions of Instructional Leadership in Assessment

Principal Lang's next focus in planning was to think about the assessment of the initiative. He explained that he knew his task was to determine and lead these actions:

▸ Confirm the success criteria of the initiative.

▸ Establish a method for monitoring the implementation of the initiative.

▸ Establish a method for continued support of implementation.

▸ Share this information with the staff.

He began the process by answering the questions from the planning chart on page 81.

▸ *What are the success criteria of the initiative?*

PRINCIPAL LANG: "When the staff began the initiative, we determined that our goal was to increase student engagement and learning through a hybrid learning approach. We knew we could measure student learning, but the engagement part could be difficult to quantify. That is why the team worked with all teachers to create our ideal school. We had to codify what engaged learning would look and sound like in our hybrid learning environment."

"This served two purposes. It allowed us to have clearly defined success criteria and it allowed for greater buy-in. Our teachers helped define our goal. They have a say in where we want to get. Our rubric will be used to define and measure our success."

"We also wanted to get our students' input. We developed a student survey to capture their feedback. We developed a series of questions that looked at engagement, ownership, the impact of face-to-face and virtual learning, collaboration, and critical thinking. We surveyed the students at the beginning of the year and will repeat it every quarter to measure the impact of our work. This will allow us to compare our student data, our observations of teachers, teacher self-reflection, and student feedback together."

Once success criteria had been determined, Principal Lang then had to determine the following:

▸ *How will the teachers know that they have implemented the initiative at a high level?*

PRINCIPAL LANG: "Once again, we are going to take advantage of our rubric. Having the teachers actively participate in its development ensured that we had a shared understanding of success. During PLCs and individual teacher conferences, we will use the rubric and other data sets we discussed, to talk about where teachers are in their progress."

Principal Lang knew that the monitoring must allow for growth. He then determined:

> ▸ *How will the teachers receive feedback regarding the progress of the implementation of the initiative?*

> ▸ *When will teachers receive feedback regarding the progress of the implementation of the initiative?*

PRINCIPAL LANG: "Feedback is crucial. We know the research behind its impact on learning. It is not only important to the learners, our teachers, but it is important to our administration team that will be monitoring our implementation of the initiative. We know that feedback is not about observing and telling the teacher about my observations. It is about observing, sharing an observation, and then asking thoughtful questions to allow the teacher to share their thinking. The more I can utilize the observation/feedback opportunities to better understand what decisions my teachers are making and why they are making them, the better equipped I am to provide them with the right supports for continued growth."

"I am just one part of the feedback support. Teachers will also be supported by our instructional and technology coaches. Their role will be to attend PLC meetings to provide strategies and supports. Also, they will work with teachers as needed to plan, co-teach, deliver demonstration lessons, and conduct observations. These will provide additional means for teachers to receive quality feedback on their progress."

But Principal Lang knew that he wanted to ensure that the support was focused on individual teacher growth and that the teachers felt active in the process. So, he then had to determine:

> ▸ *How will each teacher identify when they are succeeding and when they are struggling?*

> ▸ *What supports will the teachers receive if they are struggling?*

> ▸ *How will the teacher have a say in determining their needs?*

PRINCIPAL LANG: "During our individual meetings with teachers, we will utilize our rubric to allow teachers to explain where they are, where they have grown, what supports helped them grow, where they are struggling and what additional supports they feel they may need. This self-reflection will be coupled with our observations, coach feedback, and our students' academic and survey data. At the onset, we listened to the teachers' feedback on our plan. At each quarter, after we collect the student survey results and benchmark data, we meet together as a faculty. We review the data and our plan. We collectively decide if we need to make any changes to the plan or if we feel we are on track."

"Having said all of that, I do have some teachers that I am working with on individual support plans. Some of these plans were initiated by the teachers that came to me and let me know they needed more support. Some were teachers I identified and developed a plan with."

To ensure that his message was clearly articulated and understood, Principal Lang had to determine:

> ▸ *How will the information be shared in as many distinct ways as possible?*

PRINCIPAL LANG: "Because much of the feedback conversations were structured around me asking questions of the teachers and their decision-making, they were used to telling me their thinking and understanding. I never jumped into a conversation without first taking a few minutes to have them set the context. I would start the one-to-one conversations by asking them to put into their own words the purpose of the initiative, the expectations of the initiative, and the value to both themselves and the students. This lets me monitor their understanding and clarify broad misunderstandings, if there were any. This was important before we then discussed the details of the work. I found that without doing this, we would be going around and around about a detail when the real issue was a broad misunderstanding and that actually we were on the same page."

The Actions of Instructional Leadership in Climate

Principal Lang knew his next focus had to be on the climate of the initiative. His task was to determine and lead these actions:

▸ Identify the role of each stakeholder in the implementation of the initiative.

▸ Foster cooperation among and between stakeholders.

▸ Establish a plan for collaboration.

▸ Share this information with the staff.

He began the process by answering the questions from the planning chart on page 107.

▸ *What is the role of the teacher in the implementation of the initiative?*

▸ *What is the role of the principal in the implementation of the initiative?*

▸ *What is the role of the coach in the implementation of the initiative?*

PRINCIPAL LANG: "I see our three roles very clearly. The teachers' role is two-fold. Their primary role is to implement the initiative. They are on the front line. They are the ones receiving this new learning, adapting how they plan, learning about and implementing new technology applications, and developing stronger opportunities for our students to engage with content and each other."

"Their second role is to support each other in their PLC and department meetings. This requires them to be open about their successes and challenges and to share and support each other. This secondary role comes pretty easily to my faculty. We worked hard during our initiative on developing student ownership to build a collaborative climate. Our work will pay off now."

"My role is to monitor and support them. This means that I, and my administrative team, must understand, with clarity, where we are heading and where each individual is in their progress toward the outcome. Our instructional coaches are the bridge between us. Their role is to work with the teachers and me to identify areas of need and support them, and to identify areas of success and help us understand how to replicate them."

Once the roles had been determined, Principal Lang then had to determine the following:

> ▸ *How will the teachers be supported and encouraged to take risks in the implementation of the initiative?*

PRINCIPAL LANG: "This initiative will take our collaborative climate to a new level. This is brand new to all of us. We will not succeed if we do not take risks. We have nurtured a climate for safe and smart risk-taking. But not all teachers have had to take many risks in our previous initiatives. That will not hold true for this one. Knowing this, I need to be certain that we remind ourselves about the role of risk-taking and its impact on our learning and hence on our students' learning. I will also need to intentionally call out and celebrate our risk-taking."

Principal Lang knew that he could not do all of the work alone. He needed the teachers to work as a team. He then determined:

> ▸ *What is the purpose and value of collaborative support?*
> ▸ *What is the role of each teacher in a collaborative opportunity?*
> ▸ *When will teachers work together to support each other in the implementation of the initiative?*

PRINCIPAL LANG: "In our school, we use an analogy of rowing a boat. We know that we get farther and faster if we all row in the same direction and if we all row together. Rowing in different directions causes us to go in circles and get nowhere. When we don't all row together, a few of us get incredibly tired and we don't get very far. This is a school that has seen the benefits of collaborating."

"We will build off our collaborative mindset during our dedicated planning and PLC times. Teachers are required to plan courses together. Teachers need to think of their standards in units and develop strong final demonstrations of learning for each unit. We also need them to think about the learning process—from initial instruction of skills to practice opportunities to an authentic application to the transference of skills."

"Then, they need to consider which phases of the learning lend themselves best to in-class instruction, to synchronous learning, or to asynchronous learning. They need to consider how they will provide students with varied opportunities to collaborate with peers and to communicate their learning along the way. In addition, teachers will need to plan with the students' role in learning in mind every step of the way."

"This is work that should not be done alone. We need teachers to talk through their decisions together and justify them. We need them to work with their colleagues to bounce ideas off each other and to share successes and challenges. We have actually taken a rowboat picture that we used last year and imposed the words *hybrid learning* on top of it. We want to make certain we continue to row our boat in the same direction together!"

To ensure that his message was clearly articulated and understood, Principal Lang had to determine:

> ▸ *How will the information be shared in as many distinct ways as possible?*

PRINCIPAL LANG: "When it comes to building a professional learning climate, I realized that I needed to model everything I expected of my staff. If I expected them to share ideas, take risks, and listen to each other, I had to do the same. And I told them I was doing this. Nothing was hidden. They let me know that my transparency with communication led them to trust me and the process more."

6 DIFFERENTIATED DELEGATION

How to Ensure Individual Success

When we, as educators, hear the term *differentiation*, we think of a classroom full of students whose distinct needs are being met in a variety of ways by the teacher. Each student needs to know what they are learning, how they will show they have learned it, what strategies they can use to learn, how they will be monitored and assessed, and their role in the classroom. However, due to their distinct needs, teachers do not use a one-size-fits-all approach.

> In a differentiated classroom, the teacher assumes that different learners have differing needs and proactively plans lessons that provide a variety of way to "get at" and express learning. The teacher may still need to fin-tune instruction for some learners, but because the teacher knows the varied learner needs within the classroom and selects learning options accordingly, the chances are greater that these experiences will be an appropriate fit for most learners. (Tomlinson, 2017, p. 5)

How learning is explained, practiced, and monitored must meet the needs of each and every student learner.

The same is true for adult learners. A principal utilizing instructional leadership knows that all learning is supported by a differentiated approach to delegation based on each individual's motivation and capacity.

To that end, a principal utilizing the power of instructional leadership understands that with each new initiative, the teacher must be treated as a learner who must receive support specific to their needs. For adult learners, even those who are highly educated in the pedagogy of teaching and learning, this still holds true. Each learner needs to have their support differentiated in terms of how they understand the initiative, receive the support, and are held accountable.

Remember, effective teachers are the most important factor contributing to student achievement. You know that you need to focus on the growth of the teacher. You should respect the teacher as a learner and honor the teacher's learning process. In other words, you must differentiate the teacher's learning by strategically offering those practices that most effectively and efficiently support distinct approaches to adult learning through the actions of instructional leadership.

In the previous chapters, you have already determined the work involved in curriculum, instruction, assessment, and climate of the initiative and its successful implementation. While determining this work, you have built in a variety of supports that can be differentiated based on the needs of each and every learner.

Now, you must determine how you delegate and explain the work involved in the implementation of the initiative. You cannot delegate the work in the same way to every teacher. You must determine what is the best approach to explain the decisions, monitor these decisions, and honor the decisions of each and every teacher. Your approach to delegation must be differentiated for each and every teacher.

Differentiated delegation must take into account the teacher's approach to the initiative—their desire and energy, as well as their skill and experience. Richard F. Elmore (2004) points out that for many teachers this needs to be a personalized approach.

> It is unlikely that teachers who are not intrinsically motivated to engage in hard, uncertain work will learn to do so in large, anonymous organizations that do not intensify personal commitments and responsibilities. (p. 39)

In other words, the support is dependent on each teacher's motivation—the will, the desire, and the energy to perform well. Support is also dependent on each teacher's capacity—the skill, the capability, and the experience necessary to implement the initiative. Please note that a teacher's motivation is separate from their capacity. A high or low motivation tells the instructional leader nothing about whether a teacher has high or low capacity. An instructional leader also knows that this schema is situational and is dependent on the initiative. For example, with one task, a teacher might have low motivation but high capacity to succeed. For another, the same teacher might have high motivation and low capacity. When support in each of these instances is differentiated to meet the teacher's needs, the probability for success is increased.

> How learning is explained, practiced, and monitored must meet the needs of each and every student learner. The same is true for adult learners.

Your understanding of each teacher's motivation and capacity to implement the initiative at the highest level offers you the information to determine your approach—directing, encouraging, instructing, or clarifying. How you plan and offer your support ensures greater likelihood of successful implementation from each teacher.

When a teacher approaches the implementation of the initiative with low motivation and low capacity, instructional leadership suggests you offer differentiated support by directing.

When a teacher approaches the implementation of the initiative with low motivation and high capacity, instructional leadership suggests you offer differentiated support by encouraging.

When a teacher approaches the implementation of the initiative with high motivation and low capacity, instructional leadership suggests you offer differentiated support by instructing.

When a teacher approaches the implementation of the initiative with high motivation and high capacity, instructional leadership suggests you offer differentiated support by clarifying.

Thus, you will notice in Figure C that support falls on a continuum of more directive to less directive. You might discover that within the implementation of the initiative, a teacher's motivation and capacity change and you will need to alter your approach. For example, as you work with a teacher who initially approached the initiative with low motivation and low capacity, you might discover that, with their success, you can ease how direct your delegation needs to be and become more collaborative with decision-making.

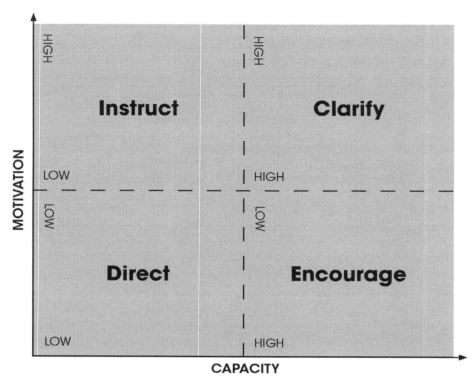

Figure C: Continuum of Motivation and Capacity
Adapted from Schemel (1997)

General Guidelines for Differentiated Delegation

When the teacher approaches the implementation of the initiative with low motivation and low capacity, instructional leadership suggests the principal **DIRECT** in order to build motivation and build capacity.

1. Explain the context of the initiative.

2. Clearly describe the outcome of the initiative.

3. Clearly describe the process of how to achieve the goal of the initiative—step by step.

4. Set dates for frequent progress checks with the teacher.

5. Provide extra help if needed—but only if needed.

6. Have the teacher reflect on their implementation of the initiative.

7. Ask the teacher what they would like to continue working on with regard to the initiative.

When the teacher approaches the implementation of the initiative with low motivation and high capacity, instructional leadership suggests the principal **ENCOURAGE** in order to build motivation and support capacity.

1. Explain the context of the initiative.

2. Clearly describe the outcome of the initiative

3. Come to an agreement with the teacher on the process of how to achieve the goal of the initiative.

4. Set dates for frequent progress checks with the teacher.

5. Ask the teacher what they would like to continue working on with regard to the initiative.

When the teacher approaches the implementation of the initiative with high motivation and low capacity, instructional leadership suggests the principal **INSTRUCT** in order to support motivation and build capacity.

1. Clearly describe the context and outcome of the initiative.

2. Clearly describe the process of how to achieve the goal of the initiative—step by step.

3. Set dates for progress checks with the teacher.

4. Allow time for implementation of the initiative and provide extra help if needed.

When the teacher approaches the implementation of the initiative with high motivation and high capacity, instructional leadership suggests the principal **CLARIFY** in order to support motivation and support capacity.

1. Clearly describe the context and outcome of the initiative and agree on time frames.

2. Ask the teacher how they will achieve the goal of the initiative and come to an agreement.

3. Check with the teacher on progress as needed.

Tables 6.1–6.4, on the following pages, offer guidance on how to differentiate support for your teachers.

Guidelines for Directing

When the teacher approaches the implementation of the initiative with low motivation and low capacity, instructional leadership suggests the principal **DIRECT** in order to build motivation and build capacity.

1. **Explain the context of the initiative.**

   What is the purpose of the initiative?

   How will the success of the initiative benefit the students?

   How will the success of the initiative benefit the teacher?

2. **Clearly describe the outcome of the initiative.**

   What, specifically, will the teacher be expected to implement?

   What, specifically, are the success criteria for the initiative?

3. **Clearly describe the process of how to achieve the goal of the initiative—step by step.**

   What specific actions does the teacher need to take?

   When do these actions need to be taken?

   What supports will the teacher receive in order to achieve the goal of the initiative?

4. Set dates for frequent progress checks with the teacher.

What are the major phases of the initiative and when should they be completed?

When will the work in progress on the initiative be reviewed?

How will the instructional leader deliver feedback? What questions will the instructional leader ask to support the teacher's decision making?

5. Provide extra help if needed—but only if needed.

Provide needed supports, but don't let the teacher's low motivation excuse them from doing the work the initiative requires.

6. Have the teacher reflect on their implementation of the initiative.

What successes have you seen? What are still some areas for growth?

How have your students benefited from the implementation of the initiative?

7. Ask the teacher what they would like to continue working on with regard to the initiative.

Help the teacher develop a plan of action for next steps.

Table 6.1: Guidelines for Directing
Adapted from Schemel (1997)

Guidelines for Encouraging

When the teacher approaches the implementation of the initiative with low motivation and high capacity, instructional leadership suggests the principal **ENCOURAGE** in order to build motivation and support capacity.

1. **Explain the context of the initiative.**

   What is the purpose of the initiative?

   How will the success of the initiative benefit the students?

   How will the success of the initiative benefit the teacher?

2. **Clearly describe the outcome of the initiative.**

   What, specifically, will the teacher be expected to implement?

   What, specifically, are the success criteria for the initiative?

3. **Come to an agreement with the teacher on the process of how to achieve the goal of the initiative.**

   Make sure the goal is clear.

   Identify what the teacher is already doing and build on their strengths.

   Agree on specific additional actions the teacher needs to take.

   Agree on when these actions need to be taken.

   Agree on the supports the teacher will receive in order to achieve the goal of the initiative.

4. Set dates for frequent progress checks with the teacher.

Mark calendars with dates for frequent reviews.

How will the instructional leader deliver feedback? What questions will the principal ask to support the teacher's decision-making?

Offer opportunities for support if needed.

5. Have the teacher reflect on their implementation of the initiative.

What successes have you seen? What are still some areas for growth?

How have your students benefited from the implementation of the initiative?

6. Ask the teacher what they would like to continue working on with regard to the initiative.

Help the teacher develop a plan of action for next steps.

Table 6.2: Guidelines for Encouraging
Adapted from Schemel (1997)

Guidelines for Instructing

When the teacher approaches the implementation of the initiative with high motivation and low capacity, instructional leadership suggests the principal **INSTRUCT** in order to support motivation and build capacity.

1. **Clearly describe the context and outcome of the initiative.**

   What is the purpose of the initiative?

   What, specifically, will the teacher be expected to implement?

   What, specifically, are the success criteria for the initiative?

2. **Clearly describe the process of how to achieve the goal of the initiative—step by step.**

   What specific actions does the teacher need to take?

   When do these actions need to be taken?

   What supports will the teacher receive in order to achieve the goal of the initiative?

3. **Set dates for progress checks with the individual.**

   What are the major phases of the initiative and when should they be completed?

   How will the principal deliver feedback?

   What questions will the instructional leader ask to support the teacher's decision-making?

4. **Allow time for implementation of the initiative and provide extra help if needed.**

   If the teacher makes mistakes, be understanding and help them learn from their mistakes.

   Ask the teacher if extra help is needed. (The teacher may need some help but their high motivation may cause reluctance to say so.)

Table 6.3: Guidelines for Encouraging
Adapted from Schemel (1997)

Guidelines for Clarifying

When the teacher approaches the implementation of the initiative with high motivation and high capacity, instructional leadership suggests the principal **CLARIFY** in order to support motivation and support capacity.

1. **Clearly describe the context and outcome of the initiative and agree on time frames.**

   What, specifically, will be the outcome of the initiative?

   What, specifically, are the success criteria for the initiative?

   When do the major phases of the initiative need to be completed?

2. **Ask the teacher how they will achieve the goal of the initiative and come to an agreement.**

   Ask the individual what specific actions they need to take.

   Ask when these actions need to be taken.

   Ask what supports the teacher would like to receive in order to achieve the goal of the initiative.

3. **Check with the teacher on progress as needed.**

   Ask the teacher when progress on the initiative should be reviewed.

   Ask the teacher how they would like to receive feedback.

Table 6.4: Guidelines for Clarifying
Adapted from Schemel (1997)

In order for you to implement a sustainable initiative, it is vital that you utilize the actions of instructional leadership and begin to see yourself as a leader whose role is to build a climate of ownership at their site.

When leaders honor their teachers by giving them the authority, the capacity, and the responsibility to implement the initiative, they see heightened motivation and enriched capacity. This increase in motivation and capacity leads to more focused decision-making, which, in turn, leads to increased support for all students.

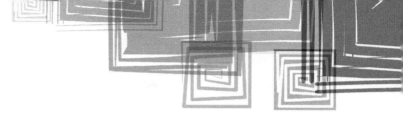

7 QUESTION-DRIVEN FEEDBACK

How to Ensure Individual Metacognition

As educators, we know the impact meaningful conversations have on learning. We know that the more opportunities students have to share ideas, clarify their thinking with others, make mistakes as they are talking, and force themselves to solidify their understanding, the greater probability they have to learn the content or skills at a deeper level. This is metacognition, and it requires learners to examine, externalize, and apply their thinking, such as:

- What it means to learn something,

- Awareness of one's strengths and weaknesses with specific skills or in a given learning context,

- Planning what's required to accomplish a specific learning goal or activity,

- Identifying and correcting errors, and

- Preparing ahead for learning processes. (Chick, 2017)

Metacognition is related to the concept of student ownership—a mindset that leads to elevated academic achievement and that teachers can develop in themselves and in their students. It is the critical thinking skills that empower students to think about, question, and communicate new learning in lasting ways (Zwiers & Crawford, 2011).

The same is true for adult learners. A principal who is utilizing instructional leadership knows that all learning is supported by a question-driven approach for monitoring and offering feedback.

Throughout this book, we have defined the actions of instructional leadership in terms of the implementation of an initiative that increases student achievement. We have shared the importance of having a thoughtful, detailed plan specific to the curriculum, instruction, assessment, and climate of the initiative. We have shared the importance of communicating every aspect of this plan over and over to ensure clarity from all stakeholders. We have shared the importance of knowing your teachers—their motivation and capacity—and how you will need to differentiate how you delegate the work. We have shared that instructional leadership is about supporting teachers to own their role in the initiative.

But this can only happen if teachers are supported to make stronger decisions. They are being asked to make changes in how they do business. They are being asked to explain how they make changes and the decision-making process behind the change. They need to be clear on the changes they are making and the decisions behind those changes. This can only happen if they are supported to build metacognition around their decisions: how they are making them, why they are making them, and the impact these changes are having on student learning.

To that end, a principal utilizing the power of instructional leadership understands that the most effective method to support stronger teachers' decision making is through a question-driven process.

> Telling or asking closed questions saves people from having to think. Asking open questions causes them to think for themselves.
> (Whitmore, 2017, p. 39)

This method of discourse allows the teacher to own the feedback process by explaining, clarifying, and reflecting on the decisions they are making to implement the actions of the initiative. In other words, it is incumbent on the principal to help teachers become more effective and efficient decision-makers regarding classroom practice by asking teachers how they make decisions and supporting their metacognition through the articulation of their thinking.

The value of this kind of feedback process is in the conversation. As a principal, the goal is clear—to create awareness and responsibility in teachers regarding the implementation of the initiative. What is said and done must reflect that goal. Thus, just demanding that teachers do something is useless. Instead, principals must ask effective questions that drive a thoughtful conversation that allows the teachers to articulate, clarify, question, and solidify the decisions they are making.

Because the most impactful initiatives are those that focus on increasing student achievement, the most effective way to monitor implementation is to observe their impact on student learning. Thus, the conversation begins with what was observed in the classroom. Questions should begin with broad brushstrokes and then increasingly focus on the details, always eliciting from the

> A principal utilizing instructional leadership knows that all learning is supported by a question-driven approach for monitoring and offering feedback.

teacher the decisions made and the reasoning behind each decision. This questioning for more detail maintains the focus of the conversation.

On the following pages are sample questions that can be used to guide these conversations. We begin with a series of questions to help the principal understand the impact of instruction on student learning at the lesson level. We then offer a series of questions specific to the implementation of individual initiatives. These questions are only a jumping-off point. As John Whitmore (2017) explains,

> Questions are most commonly asked in order to elicit information. I may require information to resolve an issue for myself, or if I am proffering advice or a solution to someone else. If I am a [principal], however, the answers are of secondary importance. The information is not for me to make use of and may not have to be complete. I only need to know that the [teacher] has the necessary information. The answers given by the [teacher] frequently indicate to the [principal] the line to follow with subsequent questions, while at the same time enabling him to monitor whether the [teacher] is following a productive track, or one that is in line with the [initiative being implemented]. (p. 41)

Therefore, give yourself the freedom to take the conversation in any direction that allows you to better understand the teacher's thinking. Remember, the aim of every conversation is to have the teacher articulate their decision-making process.

Questions to Drive Feedback at the Lesson Level

We begin our conversation at the lesson level. It is important to first understand what decisions the teacher made regarding the lesson observed. We know from Madeline Hunter (1982) that teaching is a constant stream of decisions made before, during, and after interactions with students. Each lesson must be driven by the learner, the learning outcome of the lesson, and how the learner is supported to own their learning.

There are five student-centered phases of an effective lesson.

1. **Setting the Learning Context:** Why is the learning important?

2. **Stating the Learning Outcome:** What will the students learn?

3. **Engaging in the Learning Process:** How will the students learn it?

4. **Producing the Learning Demonstration:** How will the students demonstrate that they learned it?

5. **Implementing the Learning Application:** How will the students continue to use what they have learned?

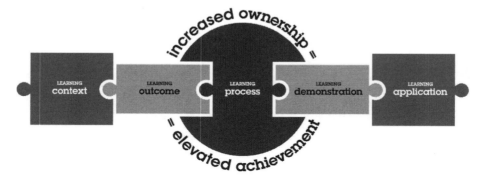

Figure D: A Learning Model That Develops Ownership

In Table 7.1 are questions you may selectively utilize to begin to understand the decisions a teacher made at the lesson level.

Questions to Drive Feedback: Lesson Level

The purpose of these questions is to support the teacher to reflect on their own decision-making at the lesson level. This thinking can be elicited by asking, "How did you decide that?" after each question.

Begin by asking broader questions:

- What were the students learning?

- What did the students do to show that they had learned it?

- Was the lesson successful for you? Were you pleased with the results?

Then, reflect on the phases of the lesson by asking more detailed questions to get a complete understanding of the teacher's thinking.

Learning Context: *Why is the learning important?*

- How did the students know the learning outcome of the lesson?

- Why were they learning this?

- How does today's learning connect to yesterday's and tomorrow's?

- How will your student use this learning in the future?

- Which resources did you use for this lesson?

- How did you decide the answers to these questions?

- How did you share this information with your students?

Learning Outcome: *What did the students learn?*

- What skill were the students learning?

- What did the students do to show that they learned this skill?

- How did the students know the learning outcome of the lesson?

- How did you decide the answers to these questions?

- How did you share this information with your students?

Learning Process: *How did the students learn it?*

- What strategy did you select to teach the skill?

- How did you share this information with your students?

- Was the strategy effective? What is you evidence?

- Were you pleased with the instructional decisions you made?

- How did you decide the answers to these questions?

Learning Demonstration: *How did the students show that they have learned it?*

- What did the students do to show that they learned the skill?

- How did you share this information with your students?

- What were the results?

- How did you decide the answers to these questions?

Learning Application: *How will the students continue to use what they learned?*

- How does today's learning connect to subsequent learning?

- How will your students use this learning in the future?

- How will your students own this learning in the future?

- How did you decide the answers to these questions?

- How did you share this information with your students?

Table 7.1: Questions to Drive Feedback at the Lesson Level

Questions to Drive Feedback at the Initiative Level

Once the teacher has been allowed to share, clarify, reflect, and restate their decision-making at the lesson level, the principal is ready to ask more detailed questions regarding the specific initiative. Again, these lists aren't exhaustive. As teachers become more comfortable with this type of feedback, the conversations will flow into a natural give and take—with the principal's role being the interested learner and the teacher's role being the articulate expert.

Questions to Drive Feedback: Initiative Level, Implementing a Course Scope and Sequence

The purpose of these questions is to support the teacher to reflect on their own decision-making regarding their implementation of the initiative. This thinking can be elicited by asking, "How did you decide that?" after each question.

- How did you use the scope and sequence to determine the outcome of the lesson?

- Why were the students learning this?

- How does today's learning connect to yesterday's and tomorrow's?

- Based on the scope and sequence, how will your students use this learning in the future?

- How is the implementation of this initiative working for you?

- What are the successes you have had?

- What are the challenges you have had?

- Is there anything I need to know regarding the implementation of this initiative?

Table 7.2: Questions to Drive Feedback at the Initiative Level, Implementing a Course Scope and Sequence

Questions to Drive Feedback: Initiative Level, Utilizing a Specific Instructional Strategy

The purpose of these questions is to support the teacher to reflect on their own decision-making regarding their implementation of the initiative. This thinking can be elicited by asking, "How did you decide that?" after each question.

- How did you decide this instructional strategy was the most effective and efficient way for the students to meet the learning outcome of the lesson?

- Did the strategy work as you had intended? Why or why not?

- What evidence did you use to determine the effectiveness of the strategy you used?

- What other instructional strategies did you select to have your students meet the learning outcome?

- What routines have you set up for your students that made this strategy more efficient?

- Do these routines work as you have intended? Why or why not?

- How is the implementation of this initiative working for you?

- What are the successes you have had?

- What are the challenges you have had?

- Is there anything I need to know regarding the implementation of this initiative?

Table 7.3: Questions to Drive Feedback at the Initiative Level, Utilizing a Specific Instructional Strategy

Questions to Drive Feedback: Initiative Level, Utilizing New Instructional Resources

The purpose of these questions is to support the teacher to reflect on their own decision-making regarding their implementation of the initiative. This thinking can be elicited by asking, "How did you decide that?" after each question.

- How did you determine the learning outcome of the lesson?

- Why were the students learning this?

- Which resources did you use for this lesson?

- How did the resources support the content and rigor of the learning outcome?

- How did you decide which resources to use with your students?

- Did the resources work as you had intended? Why or why not?

- How is the implementation of this initiative working for you?

- What are the successes you have had?

- What are the challenges you have had?

- Is there anything I need to know regarding the implementation of this initiative?

Table 7.4: Questions to Drive Feedback at the Initiative Level, Utilizing New Instructional Resources

Questions to Drive Feedback: Initiative Level, Developing Student Ownership

The purpose of these questions is to support the teacher to reflect on their own decision-making regarding their implementation of the initiative. This thinking can be elicited by asking, "How did you decide that?" after each question.

- What is the role of the student in your classroom?

- How do you ensure that students have the authority, capacity, and responsibility to own their learning?

- Were your students able to articulate what skill they were learning today, why they were learning it, and how they would show they learned it? What is your evidence?

- How did you support your students to be able to articulate what skill they were learning today, why they were learning it, and how they would show that they learned it?

- Were your students able to articulate how they were learning the skill and if they were learning or struggling? What is your evidence?

- How did you support your students to be able to articulate how they were learning the skill and if they were learning or struggling?

- How is the implementation of this initiative working for you?

- What are the successes you have had?

- What are the challenges you have had?

- Is there anything I need to know regarding the implementation of this initiative?

Table 7.5: Questions to Drive Feedback at the Initiative Level, Developing Student Ownership

Questions to Drive Feedback: Initiative Level, Implementing a Data Protocol

The purpose of these questions is to support the teacher to reflect on their own decision-making regarding their implementation of the initiative. This thinking can be elicited by asking, "How did you decide that?" after each question.

- How does this data protocol help you understand the needs of your students?

- What specific student needs did you discover through the data protocol process?

- How do you differentiate based on these needs?

- How does this data protocol help you understand what was successful in your decision-making?

- How does this data protocol help you understand what needs improvement in your decision-making?

- How is the implementation of this initiative working for you?

- What are the successes you have had?

- What are the challenges you have had?

- Is there anything I need to know regarding the implementation of this initiative?

Table 7.6: Questions to Drive Feedback at the Initiative Level, Implementing a Data Protocol

Questions to Drive Feedback: Initiative Level, Teaching through Distance Learning

The purpose of these questions is to support the teacher to reflect on their own decision-making regarding their implementation of the initiative. This thinking can be elicited by asking, "How did you decide that?" after each question.

- Which platform are you using for the online support?

- How do you decide what learning outcomes are best suited for live online instruction?

- How do you decide what learning outcomes are best suited for prerecorded online instruction?

- How do you decide what learning outcomes are best suited for at-home practice or application?

- How do you leverage distance learning to support each student's differentiated needs?

- How is the implementation of this initiative working for you?

- What are the successes you have had?

- What are the challenges you have had?

- Is there anything I need to know regarding the implementation of this initiative?

Table 7.7: Questions to Drive Feedback at the Initiative Level, Teaching through Distance Learning

Teachers play a crucial role in ensuring that students receive the positive effects of a well-implemented student-focused initiative. The teacher is the key decision-maker for establishing effective learning design before, during, and after instruction. Because the teacher is the person who knows the most about the students, it is important that the teacher's ownership in making these decisions is cultivated by the principal.

8 COMMUNICATION
How to Ensure Collective Clarity

Finally, one of the most important aspects of instructional leadership is to continuously, purposefully, and intentionally share information with the staff. This is the notion of conceptual redundancy.

> To succeed, leaders must carefully select, severely limit, and then persistently clarify (and clarify, and clarify, and clarify) the work to be done by those who lead. (Schmoker, 2016, p. 11)

In other words, if you think your staff needs to hear the information again, you're right and they do. If you think your staff does not need to hear the information again, you're wrong and they do.

This chapter is not on how to communicate but on how to overcommunicate. In his book on organizational health, Patrick Lencioni (2012) conveys the importance of overcommunication this way:

> Once a leadership team has become cohesive and worked to establish clarity and alignment around the answers to the . . . critical questions, then, and only then, can they effectively move on to the next step: communicating those answers. Or better yet, overcommunicating those answers—over and over and over and over and over and over and over.
>
> That's right, seven times. I've heard claims that employees won't believe what leaders are communicating to them until they heard it seven times. Whether the real number is five, seven, or seventy-seven, the point is that people are skeptical about what they're being told unless they hear it consistently over time. (p. 141)

The real number is dependent on the listener. You will need to convey the information as many times as needed for each specific listener to hear it and then to be able to articulate it. Remember, what you say and how you say it is less important than what they hear and how they hear it.

Create a Clear Message for Diverse Listeners

If what they hear is more important than what you say, let's take a look at our listeners. What are they listening for?

Some teachers are listening for the data—*What is the success of this initiative? What numbers can we expect after we have implemented?* These teachers won't be able to hear the entire message until they hear the data.

Some teachers are listening for the effect on people—*Who will this concern? How will this help our students? How will this help us?* These teachers won't be able to hear the entire message until they hear the effect on people.

Some teachers are listening for the big picture—*Why are we doing this? How does this connect to what we are already doing?* These teachers won't be able to hear the entire message until they hear the context of the initiative.

Some teachers are listening for the actions—*What am I going to be asked to do? What is the timeline? What is the deadline? How will I know I am doing it perfectly?* These teachers won't be able to hear the entire message until they hear the details.

When you are communicating with your audience, you must take into account the variety of listeners and address the diverse—and sometimes competing—needs of the group.

This chapter is not on how to communicate—you already have that skill or you would not be in your role as principal. You know that being as authentic as possible and being honest to yourself and your personality will take you far. However, you have just read that in

> You will need to convey the information as many times as needed for each specific listener to hear it and then to be able to articulate it. Remember, what you say and how you say it is less important than what they hear and how they hear it.

order to effectively and efficiently utilize the skills of instructional leadership, you must overcommunicate. Let's review how the principals quoted in this book did just that—overcommunicated their decisions in curriculum, instruction, assessment, and climate.

An Example of Overcommunication in Curriculum

Remember Principal Thompson? He was leading an initiative on the development of a scope and sequence at a junior high school. To ensure that his message regarding the curriculum of the initiative was clearly articulated and understood, he had to determine:

> ▶ *How will the information be shared in as many distinct ways as possible?*

PRINCIPAL THOMPSON: "I have been working hard on being more effective with communication over the last couple of years. I learned the hard way that what I say is not always what people hear. I knew that I needed to be super redundant in my communication on every level of this initiative. This meant that things needed to be repeated over and over. And not just in one manner but in lots of ways. I also make certain I put our message in writing. This allows people to read it in their voice and gives them the time to reflect on the message and the space to generate questions they may have."

"In addition, I make sure to work with the leadership team. First, we all have to be on the same page about how to discuss the initiative. We decide what to say and how we will share in the delivery of the message. This way, it is stated by many and heard by many."

An Example of Overcommunication in Instruction

Remember Principal Washington? She was leading an initiative on the implementation of a schoolwide reading strategy—reciprocal teaching. To ensure that her message regarding the instruction of the initiative was clearly articulated and understood, she had to determine:

> ▶ *How will the information be shared in as many distinct ways as possible?*

PRINCIPAL WASHINGTON: "Sharing the information regarding support for reciprocal teaching was actually quite easy. Because we had developed the support plan together, my task was to remind them of our decisions. Before every session, I ask the group two questions: 'What are the goals of the initiative?' 'How will today's session support the implementation of the initiative?' We discuss and make sure we are all on the same page. I do this before each session—even those I don't participate in. At the end of those days, I send the teachers who participated an email and ask them to reflect on the work: *What did you learn? How will this help you implement the initiative? What are your next steps?* I always end the emails with a reminder that they can request any support they feel they need. And I try my hardest to provide it for them."

An Example of Overcommunication in Assessment

Remember Principal Sanchez? She was leading an initiative on developing student ownership at her high school. To ensure that her message regarding the assessment of the initiative was clearly articulated and understood, she had to determine:

> ▸ *How will the information be shared in as many distinct ways as possible?*

PRINCIPAL SANCHEZ: "I shared earlier how I realized that we internalize information differently. Knowing this, I could not just share the plan and hope that everyone would hear it the same way. Codifying our initiative and success criteria helped us tremendously to ensure that we were in agreement. I have shared a copy of it with every teacher and I bring this out in every feedback session. We always start our conversation by reviewing it. I know it is important that we always keep the context and goal in mind."

An Example of Overcommunication in Climate

Remember Principal Balsamo? He was leading an initiative to implement a data protocol. To ensure that his message regarding the climate of the initiative was clearly articulated and understood, he had to determine:

> ▸ *How will the information be shared in as many distinct ways as possible?*

PRINCIPAL BALSAMO: "There were parts of the initiative that I shared with the staff and parts that I needed them to determine. Even when I shared a part—for example, the goal and success criteria of the data analysis protocol—I made certain they had time to discuss it and then articulate it in their own words. An example of the part I needed them to determine was what their role would be in a PLC meeting. We outlined the purpose and value of the meetings. I then had the teachers come up with what would be their role, what was expected of each individual, and what was expected of the group."

"We also use each staff meeting as a time to remind ourselves about our initiative and then to check in on our progress. I have found that this level of consistent communication and articulation has helped us become what we wanted: a school of 'we' rather than a school of individual 'I's."

An Example of Overcommunication When Implementing a Hybrid Learning Model

Remember Principal Lang? He was leading an initiative at his elementary school focused on the implementation of a hybrid learning model that combines the effectiveness and socialization opportunities of direct teacher instruction in the classroom and the robust active learning opportunities offered through technology. To ensure that his message regarding the curriculum, instruction, assessment, and climate of the initiative was clearly articulated and understood, he had to determine for each area how he will share the information with the staff.

> ▸ *How will the information for curriculum be shared in as many distinct ways as possible?*

PRINCIPAL LANG: "I learned a great deal when we communicated our initiative for the first time. No one got it. To put it in perspective, I remember teachers telling me that students seemed oblivious to their learning goals and plans."

"'But I told them!' they would say. 'Why are they saying they don't know?'"

"I realized that I actually did the same thing. I even said to them, 'But I told you! Why are you saying you didn't know?'"

"How embarrassing. Well, by grappling with this issue, we learned that just saying something once does not mean everyone understood or even heard it. We learned that, just like with students, the teachers needed to articulate it, in their own words, and more than once. So, I now do the same thing. As I share information, I have the teachers first talk to each other to put it in their own words and then share it with all of us. This allows us to know whether or not everyone has the same message. And if not, we can clarify as needed."

> ▶ *How will the information for instruction be shared in as many distinct ways as possible?*

PRINCIPAL LANG: "I never began a meeting or conversation with a teacher without quickly reviewing the basics of the initiative. I used every opportunity to remind everyone of what we agreed we were implementing and why. This allowed teachers to hear it again and again and in a variety of situations. Because teachers are getting support in a variety of ways—initial professional development, working in small groups, or one-to-one—allowed me, the admin team, or the instructional coaches to repeat the context for the initiative, the outcome of the initiative, or the expectations of the initiative, as many times as possible."

> ▶ *How will the information for assessment be shared in as many distinct ways as possible?*

PRINCIPAL LANG: "Because much of the feedback conversations were structured around me asking questions of the teachers and their decision-making, they were used to telling me their thinking and understanding. I never jumped into a conversation without first taking a few minutes to have them set the context. I would start the one-to-one conversations by asking them to put into their own words the purpose of the initiative, the expectations of the initiative, and the value to both themselves and the students. This let me monitor their understanding and clarify broad misunderstandings, if there were any. This was important before we then discussed the details of the work. I found that without doing this, we would be going around and around about a detail when the real issue was a broad misunderstanding and that actually we were on the same page."

> ▶ *How will the information for climate be shared in as many distinct ways as possible?*

PRINCIPAL LANG: "When it comes to building a professional learning climate, I realized that I needed to model everything I expected of my staff. If I expected them to share ideas, take risks, and listen to each other, I had to do the same. And I told them I was doing this. Nothing was hidden. They let me know that my transparency with communication led them to trust me and the process more."

The Notion of Conceptual Redundancy

Again, this chapter is not about how to communicate. You will have noticed that this chapter is focused on how to overcommunicate to diverse listeners so that you don't fall into the trap that many business leaders do.

> Leaders inadvertently do the same thing when they walk away from an annual all hands-meeting and think that they've done their job of communicating by giving a speech outlining the organization's strategy or priorities. And they think they've been especially thorough when they announce that the slides for the presentation can be found on the company's intranet site. But then they seem surprised when they learn a few weeks later that employees aren't acting on what they were told and that most of those employees can't even repeat the organization's new strategy accurately.
>
> The problem is the leaders confuse the mere transfer of information to an audience with the audience's ability to understand, internalize, and embrace the message that is being communicated. (Lencioni, 2012, p. 142)

As educators, we inherently know that clear communication is the cornerstone of learning. Therefore, we are called to utilize this aspect of instructional leadership continuously, purposefully, and intentionally as we share information with each and every listener—the one listening for the data, the one listening for the people, the one listening for the big picture, the one listening for the actionable items. And if you want to know if your teachers have heard your message clearly and accurately, just ask them. Their answers will tell you.

This is the notion of conceptual redundancy. This ensures collective clarity and ultimately success.

CONCLUSION

The Power of Reflective Practice

Imagine walking into a classroom and finding students who were able to explain what they are learning, why they are learning it, and what ultimate success looks like. Imagine a school where kids loved learning and could explain their plan for achieving higher and higher year by year. Imagine talking with teachers who were able to articulate the schoolwide initiatives to increase student achievement and their specific role in them. Imagine walking into a meeting and seeing teachers working with their colleagues to clarify their understanding of the initiative and sharing their strengths and struggles. Imagine a school where teachers asked for help and support from the principal.

Can you imagine that this school is your school?

We can.

Educators know that motivation is the key to greater success. We believe that motivation can be taught. We have shown how any principal can increase staff motivation, and thus achievement, by increasing ownership.

Throughout this book we have:

▶ Defined ownership,

▶ Explained what it could look like and sound like in a variety of initiatives,

▶ Identified the principal's role in developing schoolwide ownership, and

▶ Determined the most critical actions of instructional leadership.

Using a variety of research about learning and, more specifically, adult learning, we provided you with a set of strategic learning practices that form the foundation of the clear and consistent actions the principal must take to support their teachers' ownership of their learning to ensure successful implementation of the initiative. In other words, the strategic learning practices translate into the four actions of instructional leadership.

How does a principal do this? Remember, principals model the thinking behind the ownership and explicitly address the skills of ownership. This takes planning. In order for all stakeholders to successfully support an initiative focused on increasing student achievement, principals must be strategic in the actions they use to support staff.

While there are hundreds of actions a principal must take in a day, this book focused on those practices and actions in curriculum, instruction, assessment, and climate that actually increase the opportunities for learning—and increase the opportunities for ownership. The strategic learning practices and actions of instructional leadership in each area are as follows.

> Educators know that motivation is the key to greater success. We believe that motivation can be taught. We have shown how any principal can increase staff motivation, and thus achievement, by increasing ownership.

Curriculum Support

All support and learning is driven by a clearly defined initiative with measurable and achievable outcomes.

The Practices That Drive Instructional Leadership in Curriculum

- **Strategic Learning Practice, Curriculum 1:** Adults are supported by relevant expectations with measurable and achievable outcomes that are accessible and drive all learning.

- **Strategic Learning Practice, Curriculum 2:** Adults are supported by a plan for learning that provides an integrated approach and that supports conceptual redundancy of the outcomes.

- **Strategic Learning Practice, Curriculum 3:** Adults are supported by access to materials that match the content and rigor of the outcomes.

In other words . . .

1. When teachers clearly understand the goal of the initiative, they have a better chance to be successful.

2. When teachers clearly understand how the work of the initiative is integrated into their current work, they have a better chance to be successful.

3. When teachers have access to appropriate and relevant resources, they have a better chance to be successful.

Which translates into . . .

The Actions of Instructional Leadership in Curriculum

▸ Clarify the goals of the initiative.

▸ Integrate the goals of the initiative with other expectations.

▸ Provide the resources needed to implement the initiative.

▸ *Share this information with the staff.*

Instruction Support

All support and learning is driven by highly engaging, effective, and efficient instruction.

The Practices That Drive Instructional Leadership in Instruction

- **Strategic Learning Practice, Instruction 1:** Adults are supported by opportunities for meaningful engagement using structured learner-to-learner communication.

- **Strategic Learning Practice, Instruction 2:** Adults are supported by opportunities for meaningful engagement using highly effective instructional strategies.

- **Strategic Learning Practice, Instruction 3:** Adults are supported by opportunities for meaningful engagement where instructional time is used efficiently.

In other words . . .

1. When teachers have opportunities for meaningful engagement using structured learner-to-learner communication, they have a better chance to be successful.

2. When teachers have opportunities for meaningful engagement using highly effective instructional strategies, they have a better chance to be successful.

3. When teachers have opportunities for meaningful engagement where instructional time is used efficiently, they have a better chance to be successful.

Which translates into . . .

The Actions of Instructional Leadership in Instruction

▸ Clarify how the initiative will be supported and implemented.

▸ Establish a plan for professional learning opportunities.

▸ Schedule professional learning opportunities directly related to the initiative.

▸ ***Share this information with the staff.***

Assessment Support

All support and learning is driven by regular assessment that guides decision-making.

The Practices That Drive Instructional Leadership in Assessment

• **Strategic Learning Practice, Assessment 1:** Adults are supported by data that is used to monitor current understanding and provide feedback.

• **Strategic Learning Practice, Assessment 2:** Adults are supported by data that is used to monitor current understanding and adjust as needed.

• **Strategic Learning Practice, Assessment 3:** Adults are supported by data that is used to differentiate based on predetermined needs.

In other words . . .

1. When teachers clearly understand the data that is used to monitor current understanding and provide feedback, they have a better chance to be successful.

2. When teachers clearly understand the data that is used to monitor current understanding and adjust as needed, they have a better chance to be successful.

3. When teachers clearly understand the data that is used to differentiate based on their individual needs, they have a better chance to be successful.

Which translates into . . .

The Actions of Instructional Leadership in Assessment

▶ Confirm the success criteria of the initiative.

▶ Establish a method for monitoring the implementation of the initiative.

▶ Establish a method for continued support of implementation.

▶ *Share this information with the staff.*

Climate Support

All support and learning is driven by a positive climate.

The Practices That Drive Instructional Leadership in Climate

- **Strategic Learning Practice, Climate 1:** Adults are supported by a respectful environment that recognizes and promotes professional behavior.

- **Strategic Learning Practice, Climate 2:** Adults are supported by a cooperative environment that encourages risk-taking.

- **Strategic Learning Practice, Climate 3:** Adults are supported by a collaborative environment that enhances individual productivity.

In other words . . .

1. When teachers are supported by a respectful environment that recognizes and promotes professional behavior, they have a better chance to be successful.

2. When teachers are supported by a cooperative environment that encourages risk-taking, they have a better chance to be successful.

3. When teachers are supported by a collaborative environment that enhances individual productivity, they have a better chance to be successful.

Which translates into . . .

The Actions of Instructional Leadership in Climate

▸ Identify the role of each stakeholder in the implementation of the initiative.

▸ Foster cooperation among and between stakeholders.

▸ Establish a plan for collaboration.

▸ *Share this information with the staff.*

Reflect on the Support You Are Providing

The degree to which you offer these strategic learning practices, through the actions of instructional leadership, determines the degree to which teachers struggle or succeed regarding the implementation of the initiative. You have the control. And, you have the greatest influence.

> Without a competent caring individual in the principal's position, the task of school reform is very difficult. Reform can be initiated from outside the school or stimulated from within. But in the end, it is the principal who implements and sustains the changes through the inevitable roller coaster of euphoria and setbacks. (Gerstner, Semerad, Doyle, & Johnston, 1994, p. 133)

The charts on the following pages show examples of strong support contrasted with examples of little to no support. Where do you fall?

You might have begun your career thinking a principal's job was to be a manager of work. But what you should notice as you read this book is that your role is really that of a reflective practitioner—the lead reflective practitioner of the school.

Reflect on the Support for Curriculum

When implementing the initiative and owning their learning in curriculum, teachers are more likely to . . .

SUCCEED, *if . . .*	STRUGGLE, *if . . .*
• They know what the initiative is and how they will know they have implemented it at a high level	• They don't know what the initiative is or how they will know they have implemented it at a high level
• They are told what they need to learn to implement the initiative	• They aren't told what they need to learn to implement the initiative
• They are learning the appropriate skills to support the implementation of the initiative	• They aren't learning the appropriate skills to support the implementation of the initiative
• The sequence of support leads to effective and efficient implementation	• The sequence of support doesn't lead to effective and efficient implementation
• Support time is focused on the skill to be learned	• Support time isn't focused on the skill to be learned
• They can hear about, talk about, read about, and write about their learning	• They aren't provided opportunities to hear about, talk about, read about, and write about their learning
• They have multiple opportunities to practice the skill in a variety of situations—during professional learning, with a coach, with colleagues, with students	• They don't have multiple opportunities to practice the skill in a variety of situations—during professional development, with a coach, with colleagues, with students
• Resources support the initiative	• Resources don't support the initiative
• Resources directly align to the implementation	• Resources aren't directly aligned to the implementation
• Resources challenge their thinking	• Resources don't challenge their thinking

Table C.1: Reflect on the Support for Curriculum

Reflect on the Support for Instruction

When implementing the initiative and owning their learning in instruction, teachers are more likely to . . .

SUCCEED, *if* . . .	STRUGGLE, *if* . . .
• They are given multiple opportunities to talk about implementation	• They are given few opportunities to talk about implementation
• Discussions are purposeful and engage the learner	• Discussions aren't purposeful and don't engage the learner
• They get to share their thinking with others implementing the initiative	• They don't get to share their thinking with others implementing the initiative
• They know why they need to interact with their colleagues	• They don't know why they need to interact with their colleagues
• They are given multiple opportunities to engage in the learning	• They are given few opportunities to engage in the learning
• Support is purposeful and engages them	• Support is not purposeful and doesn't engage them
• Support strategies lead to mastery and a deeper understanding of the initiative	• Support strategies do not lead to mastery or a deeper understanding of the initiative
• They know how to utilize the strategy effectively with students	• They don't know how to utilize the strategy effectively with students
• They have dedicated time to reflect on their own learning—what works for them, how, and why	• They don't have dedicated time to reflect on their own learning—what works for them, how, and why
• Meeting time is focused and uninterrupted	• Meeting time is unfocused and disjointed
• Dedicated meeting time is purposeful and engages them	• Dedicated meeting time is not purposeful and doesn't engage them
• The amount of time is appropriate for the learning of the skill	• Time (too much or too little) is inappropriate for the learning of the skill

Table C.2: Reflect on the Support for Instruction

Reflect on the Support for Assessment

When implementing the initiative and owning their learning in assessment, teachers are more likely to . . .

SUCCEED, *if* . . .	STRUGGLE, *if* . . .
• They have multiple opportunities to check their own understanding	• They don't have opportunities to check their own understanding
• Implementation data (positive or negative) is used to support growth	• Implementation data (positive or negative) is ignored
• They receive feedback that tells them they are on track	• They don't receive feedback that tells them they are on track
• They receive feedback that clarifies their misunderstanding	• They don't receive feedback that clarifies their misunderstanding
• They receive feedback that redirects them when they are off track	• They don't receive feedback that redirects them when they are off track
• Implementation data is gathered through a question-driven process	• Implementation data is only gathered through observation and feedback is expressed by definitive statements
• Their struggle is honored	• Their struggle is ignored
• Their specific needs are honored	• Their specific needs are ignored
• They receive support that is specific to them	• They don't receive support that is specific to them
• Differentiated support is utilized to build equity of implementation	• Everything is the same for everyone based on a false notion of equity

Table C.3: Reflect on the Support for Assessment

Reflect on the Support for Climate

When implementing the initiative and owning their learning in climate, teachers are more likely to . . .

SUCCEED, *if* . . .	STRUGGLE, *if* . . .
• The teacher is respected by administration or colleagues	• The teacher is disrespected by administration or colleagues
• The school environment is built on respect, cooperation, and collaboration	• The school environment is built on friction, cliquishness, apathy, or disorganization
• Teachers and their needs are honored	• Teachers and their needs are ignored
• Teachers have multiple opportunities to work with others	• Teachers only have the opportunity to work on their own
• Teachers are expected to make mistakes	• Teachers are reprimanded for making mistakes during implementation
• Teachers are honored for taking risks during implementation	• Teachers are not allowed to take risks
• Teachers are in a school that values individual growth over compliance	• Teachers are in a school that only values compliance and not individual growth
• Teachers work together	• Teachers cannot work together
• Teachers know the value of working together effectively	• Teachers don't know the value of working together effectively

Table C.4: Reflect on the Support for Climate

Instructional Leadership Is Driven by Reflective Practice

As you are utilizing the actions of instructional leadership to drive your initiative, you could be viewing your role as principal in a different light. You might have begun your career thinking a principal's job was to be a manager of work. But what you should notice as you read this book is that your role is really that of a reflective practitioner—the lead reflective practitioner of the school.

We have shown that the actions of instructional leadership can only be successful if driven by a leader who is willing to reflect on their role, their strengths, and their areas of growth. We have shown that a principal cannot increase student achievement alone but must harness the knowledge and skills of all. This role is in contrast to the more traditional view of a principal being the manager of work, with the implication being that they are an expert in everything and have all of the right answers.

Now, think about your experiences. Reflect on all of the principals you have worked with in the past. Were they more of a leader or the boss? Which approach gained the greatest results?

A Leader *is perceived as a reflective practitioner*	The Boss *is perceived as an expert*
• I am presumed to know, but I am not the only one in the situation to have relevant and important knowledge. My uncertainties may be a source of learning for me and for them.	• I am presumed to know, and must claim to do so, regardless of my own uncertainty.
• Seek out connections to the teacher's thoughts and feelings. Allow their understanding of my knowledge to emerge from their discovery of it in the situation.	• Keep a professional distance from the teacher and hold on to the expert's role. Give the teacher a sense of my expertise but convey a feeling of warmth and sympathy as a "sweetener."
• Look for the sense of freedom and of real connection to the teacher as a consequence of no longer needing to maintain an expert façade.	• Look for deference and status in the teacher's response to my professional persona.

Table C.5: A Leader and the Boss. Adapted from *The Reflective Practitioner*, Donald A. Schön, 1983

How Instructional Leadership Elevates Achievement

It is clear that the job of being a principal is hard work. You come to school each day motivated to provide your staff and your students with the highest quality support you can. But achievement can't be elevated if only the principal is motivated. You must ensure that your staff is motivated to be active participants in the work. Taking ownership motivates everyone to elevate their achievement in all areas—and not just motivated for the individual needs of their classroom but motivated for the collective good of all students' achievement. In this book, we have shown that building this motivation is something you control.

In order for you to implement a sustainable initiative, you must utilize the actions of instructional leadership to build a climate of ownership at your site. Research shows that you must honor the teachers by giving them the authority, capacity, and responsibility to implement the initiative. You do this by not only developing a plan that includes all facets of curriculum, instruction, assessment, and climate but also by differentiating how you delegate the work and how you communicate the work. These actions lead to professional motivation, which leads to more focused decision-making, which, in turn, leads to increased achievement for all students.

Let's revisit that dream school. This is a clear example of a school where students, teachers, and administrators are all pulling together to increase learning. Each owns their role in the process. Each is supported by another—teachers support each and every student, administration supports each and every teacher, and they all support their colleagues.

Your dream school can be a reality because you control that reality.

ADDENDUM

How District Administrators Can Support Their Principals

Dear district-level administrator, up to this point, the focus of this book has been on the actions a school-site principal can take to develop their own instructional leadership. We have shown that instructional leadership is the key to supporting all stakeholders. We have shown that the task of the principal is to lead the initiatives that will increase student achievement. And we have shared the strategic learning practices and actions of instructional leadership that principals can use to support their teachers when implementing these initiatives at the highest level.

However, the practices and actions aren't just for use with principals and their teachers. They can be used by anyone who is supporting someone else's learning. When a principal is leading the implementation of an initiative, they, too, need support. This support needs to come from their supervisor, the district administrator.

Thus, we all have a role in supporting our students.

The Spheres of Support

Consider the spheres of support as you think about your district. If a district is truly student-centered, then each educational stakeholder in the system has very specific responsibilities. These responsibilities identify the vital and unique roles of teachers, principals, and district-level administrators.

The vital role of teachers is to consistently and intentionally support students to own their learning. The vital role of school-site administrators is to consistently and intentionally support teachers to own their role in student learning. The vital role of district-level administrators is to consistently and intentionally support principals to own their role in the development of the actions of instructional leadership.

Figure A: The Spheres of Support

Thus, just like with principals, of all the skills a district administrator needs to succeed, the most vital in terms of increasing academic achievement is that of instructional leadership. The skill of instructional leadership is made up of actions that can be seen and heard. And we believe that the actions of instructional leadership can be developed and should be developed at all levels in a district.

The Power of Instructional Leadership at the District Level

What is leadership? If you were to look up this word, you would find myriad definitions. But, regardless of the intent or details of the wording, most definitions will identify leadership in some form or fashion as *the art of inspiring a group of people toward achieving a common goal.* This reminds us that regardless of the business being led, leadership is linked to a goal. It is no different in education. So, when we talk about leadership in the context of education, we know we are talking about the art of inspiring a group of people toward achieving a common set of goals for learning and academic achievement.

However, we are less concerned with a definition and more concerned with the practical answer to the question, "What are the actions of a district administrator who effectively supports a principal who leads a school with the performance outcome of increased academic achievement for each and every student?"

In other words, "What are the actions of instructional leadership?" For us, the actions of instructional leadership fall into the four categories addressed in this book—curriculum, instruction, assessment, and climate. Earlier in this book, we articulated what those actions look like and sound like when they are utilized. We also shared that instructional leadership takes into account the motivation and the capacity of the learner to implement the work. In addition, we made the case that the most efficient way to understand the thinking behind a learner's approach is to ask questions.

The purpose of this book is to clarify for you the actions of instructional leadership. If these actions are followed, you will be exemplifying the skills of instructional leadership, and, thus, you will be a district administrator who supports each and every principal to lead a school with the stated performance outcome of increasing academic achievement for all students.

> The vital role of district-level administrators is to consistently and intentionally support principals to own their role in the development of the actions of instructional leadership.

There are different types of initiatives that could be implemented in a district. Some might be at the district level—all English teachers are expected to follow the newly created scope and sequence, each math class will be using the newly purchased resources, or course-alike teacher cohorts will analyze student data using the district assessments. Some might be at the school level, based on specific site needs—the instructional strategy of reciprocal teaching will be used with English learners, the mathematical practices will be a focus in our pre-algebra and algebra classes, or blended learning activities will be developed for the student population with special needs.

With both types of initiatives, your task is to support your principals. If the initiative is district-based, your task as a district administrator is to direct and support your principals as they lead the implementation of this initiative. If the initiative is site-based, your task as a district administrator is to monitor and support your principals as they lead the implementation of a school-based initiative.

In either case, the actions of instructional leadership can be organized into a framework with four categories and are undergirded by the understanding that all support and learning is driven by:

- A clearly defined initiative with measurable and achievable outcomes

- Highly engaging, effective, and efficient instruction

- Regular assessment that guides decision-making

- A positive climate

Within this framework are the actions of instructional leadership in the areas of curriculum, instruction, assessment, and climate that you must take if an initiative is to be implemented at the highest level.

Figure B: A Learning Framework That Develops Ownership

The Actions of Instructional Leadership at the District Level

Curriculum:

- ▸ Clarify the goals of the initiative.
- ▸ Integrate the goals of the initiative with other expectations.
- ▸ Provide the resources needed to implement the initiative.
- ▸ Share this information with the principal.

Instruction:

- ▸ Clarify how the initiative will be supported and implemented.
- ▸ Establish a plan for professional learning opportunities.
- ▸ Schedule professional learning opportunities directly related to the initiative.
- ▸ Share this information with the principal.

Assessment:

- ▸ Confirm the success criteria of the initiative.
- ▸ Establish a method for monitoring the implementation of the initiative.
- ▸ Establish a method for continued support of implementation.
- ▸ Share this information with the principal.

Climate:

- ▸ Identify the role of the principal in the implementation of the initiative.
- ▸ Foster cooperation and collaboration between principals.
- ▸ Encourage risk-taking with the principal.
- ▸ Share this information with the principal.

What follows is a series of guides and planning questions to help you, as a district administrator, support the implementation of the actions of instructional leadership in each of the four areas. If the initiative is district-based, use these guides to help you determine the actions of implementation and then share your decisions with your principals. If the initiative is site-based, use these guides to help you monitor the actions of implementation and then drive conversations with your principals.

Questions to Guide Implementing the Actions of Instructional Leadership in Curriculum

All support and learning is driven by a clearly defined initiative with measurable and achievable outcomes.

Use these planning questions to focus your support.

Clarify the goals of the initiative.

❑   What are the goals of the initiative?

❑   What is the purpose of the initiative?

❑   What, specifically, will the principal be expected to lead?

❑   What, specifically, will the teacher be expected to implement?

❑   What, specifically, are the success criteria for the initiative?

❑   How will the success of the initiative benefit the students?

❑   How will the success of the initiative benefit the teachers?

❑   How will the success of the initiative benefit the principal?

Integrate the goals of the initiative with other expectations.

❑   How does the initiative support the other work the principal is leading?

Provide the resources needed to implement this initiative.

❑   What resources will the principal need to effectively lead the implementation of the initiative?

Share this information with the principal.

❑   How will the information be shared with the principal in as many distinct ways as possible?

Table A.1: Questions to Guide Implementing the Actions of Instructional Leadership in Curriculum at the District Level

Questions to Guide Implementing the Actions of Instructional Leadership in Instruction

All support and learning is driven by highly engaging, effective, and efficient instruction.

Use these planning questions to focus your support.

Clarify how the initiative will be supported and implemented.

❑ What supports will the principal receive in order to achieve the goal of the initiative?

Establish a plan for professional learning opportunities.

❑ What is the expectation of the principal for each provided support?

❑ How will the principal ask for and receive additional support?

❑ How will district principals work together to implement the initiative?

❑ How will each individual principal have opportunities to contribute ideas to the implementation plan?

Schedule professional learning opportunities directly related to the initiative.

❑ What is the timeline and plan for the initiative?

❑ When will the principal receive support?

❑ What are the milestone expectations for the principal?

Share this information with the principal.

❑ How will this information be shared in as many distinct ways as possible?

Table A.2: Questions to Guide Implementing the Actions of Instructional Leadership in Instruction at the District Level

Questions to Guide Implementing the Actions of Instructional Leadership in Assessment

All support and learning is driven by regular assessment that guides decision-making.

Use these planning questions to focus your support.

Confirm the success criteria for the initiative.

- ❑ What are the success criteria of the initiative?

- ❑ How will the principal know that the initiative has been implemented at a high level?

Establish a method for monitoring the implementation of the initiative.

- ❑ How will the principal receive feedback regarding the progress of the implementation of the initiative?

- ❑ When will the principal receive feedback regarding the progress of the implementation of the initiative?

Establish a method for continued support of implementation.

- ❑ How will the principal identify when they are succeeding and when they are struggling?

- ❑ What supports will the principal receive if they are struggling?

- ❑ How will the principal have a say in determining their needs?

Share this information with the principal.

- ❑ How will this information be shared in as many distinct ways as possible?

Table A.3: Questions to Guide Implementing the Actions of Instructional Leadership in Assessment at the District Level

Questions to Guide Implementing the Actions of Instructional Leadership in Climate

All support and learning is driven by a positive climate.

Use these planning questions to focus your support.

Identify the role of each principal in the implementation of the initiative.

❑ What is the role of the principal in the implementation of the initiative?

❑ How will the principal determine the roles of the other stakeholders at the site?

Foster cooperation among and between district principals.

❑ What is the purpose and value of cooperative and collaborative support?

❑ What is the role of each principal in these cooperative and collaborative opportunities?

❑ How will district principals work together to support each other in the implementation of the initiative?

❑ When will district principals work together to support each other in the implementation of the initiative?

Encourage risk-taking with the principal.

❑ How will the principal be supported and encouraged to take risks in the implementation of the initiative?

Share this information with the principal.

❑ How will this information be shared in as many distinct ways as possible?

Table A.4: Questions to Guide Implementing the Actions of Instructional Leadership in Climate at the District Level

REFERENCES

Alberti, S. (2013). Making the shifts. *Education Leadership, 70*(4), 24–27.

Barth, R. S. (1996) *The principal learner: Work in progress.* Cambridge, MA: International Network for Principals' Centres, Harvard Graduate School of Education.

Beck, I. L., McKeown, M. G., & Kucan, L. (2013). *Bringing words to life: Robust vocabulary instruction* (2nd ed.). New York, NY: Guilford Press.

Boucher, D. (2018). *Encouraging student self-reflection.* Retrieved from https://www .mathcoachscorner.com/2016/10/student-self-reflection/

Burns, M., & Lawrie, J. (2017). 7 recommendations to improve teacher professional development in fragile contexts. *GPE Transforming Education.* Retrieved from: https://www.globalpartnership.org/blog/7-recommendations-improve-teacher -professional-development-fragile-contexts

California Department of Education. (2013a). *California Common Core State Standards for English language arts and literacy in history/social studies, science, and technical subjects.* Sacramento, CA: Author.

California Department of Education. (2013b). *California Common Core State Standards for mathematics.* Sacramento, CA: Author.

California Department of Education. (2013c). *Overview of the standards chapters of the mathematics framework for California public schools: Kindergarten through grade twelve.* Sacramento, CA: Author. Retrieved from https://www.cde.ca.gov /Ci/ma/cf/documents/mathfwoverview.pdf

Chan, P., Graham-Day, K. J., & Ressa, V. A. (2014). Beyond involvement: Promoting student ownership of learning in classrooms. *Intervention in School and Clinic, 50*(2), 105–113.

Chick, N. (2017). Metacognition. *CFT teaching guides.* Retrieved from https:// cft.vanderbilt.edu/guides-sub-pages/metacognition/

Cohen, E. G. (1986). *Designing groupwork: Strategies for heterogeneous classrooms.* New York, NY: Teachers College Press.

Cohen, E. G., & Chatfield, M. (1991). *Complex instruction implementation manual.* Palo Alto, CA: Stanford University.

Cohen, E. G., Lotan, R. A., Whitcomb, J. A., Balderrama, M. V., Cossey, R., & Swanson, P. E. (1995). Complex instruction: Higher order thinking in heterogeneous classrooms. In R. J. Stahl (Ed.), *Handbook of cooperative learning.* Westport, CT: Greenwood.

Cohen, E. G., & Lotan, R. A. (1997). *Working for equity in heterogeneous classrooms: Sociological theory in practice.* New York, NY: Teachers College Press.

Cohen, E. G., Lotan, R. A., & Leechor, C. (1989). Can classrooms learn? *Sociology of Education, 62*(2), 75–94.

Collins, J. (2001). *Good to great.* New York, NY: HarperBusiness.

Cornelius-White, J. (2007). Learner-centered teacher-student relationships are effective: A meta-analysis. *Review of Educational Research, 77*(1), 113–143.

Crowe, R., & Kennedy, J. (2018). *Developing student ownership: Supporting students to own their learning through the use of strategic learning practices.* West Palm Beach, FL: Learning Sciences International.

Datta, D. K., & Narayanan, V. K. (1989). A meta-analytic review of the concentration-performance relationship: Aggregating findings in strategic management. *Journal of Management, 15*(3), 469–483.

Deal, T. E., & Peterson, K. D. (1999). *Shaping school culture: The heart of leadership.* San Francisco, CA: Jossey-Bass.

Dunn, R., Griggs, S. A., Olson, J., Beasley, M., & Gorman, B. S. (1995). A meta-analytic validation of the Dunn and Dunn model of learning-style preferences. *Journal of Educational Research, 88*(6), 353–362.

Dusek, J. B., & Joseph, G. (1985). The bases of teacher expectancies. In J. B. Dusek (Ed.), *Teacher expectancies* (pp. 229–249). Hillsdale, NJ: Lawrence Erlbaum Associates.

Duzinski, G. A. (1987). *The educational utility of cognitive behavior modification strategies with children: A quantitative synthesis* (Unpublished doctoral dissertation). University of Illinois at Chicago.

Elmore, R. F. (1992). Why restructuring alone won't improve teaching. *Educational Leadership, 49*(7), 44–48.

Elmore, R. F. (2004). *School reform from the inside out: Policy, practice, and performance.* Cambridge, MA: Harvard Education Press.

Emeny, W. (2013). Metacognition...Thoughts on teaching mathematical problem solving skills. Retrieved from http://www.greatmathsteachingideas.com/2013/07/23/metacognition-thoughts-on-teaching-mathematical-problem-solving-skills/

Fendick, F. (1990). *The correlation between teacher clarity of communication and student achievement gain: A meta-analysis* (Unpublished doctoral dissertation). University of Florida.

Friesen, S. (2008). *Effective teaching practices—A practice.* Toronto, Canada: Canadian Education Association.

Fuchs, L. S., & Fuchs, D. (1986a). Curriculum-based assessment of progress toward long-term and short-term goals. *Journal of Special Education, 20*(1), 69–82.

Fuchs, L. S., & Fuchs, D. (1986b). Effects of systematic formative evaluation: A meta-analysis. *Exceptional Children, 53*(3), 199–208.

Fullan, M., & Quinn, J. (2016). *Coherence: The right drivers in action for schools, districts, and systems.* Thousand Oaks, CA: Corwin Press.

Gerstner, L. V., Semerad, R. D., Doyle, D. P., & Johnston, W. B. (1994). *Reinventing education: Entrepreneurship in America's public schools.* New York, NY: Plume-Penguin.

Guskey, T. R. (2003). How classroom assessments improve learning. *Educational Leadership, 60*(5), 6–11.

Haertel, G. D., Walberg, H. J.,& Haertel, E. H. (1980). Classroom socio-psychological environments and learning: A quantitative synthesis. *British Educational Research Journal, 7*(1), 27–36.

Hammond, Z. (2015). *Culturally responsive teaching & the brain: Promoting authentic engagement and rigor among culturally and linguistically diverse students.* Thousand Oaks, CA: Corwin Press.

Hanover Research. (2014). *The impact of formative assessment and learning interventions on student achievement* [White paper]. Retrieved from Hanover Research District Administration Practice: https://www.hanoverresearch.com/media/The-Impact-of-Formative-Assessment-and-Learning-Intentions-on-Student-Achievement.pdf

Hart, B., & Risley, T. R. (1995). *Meaningful differences in the everyday experience of young American children.* Baltimore, MD: Paul H. Brookes Publishing.

Hattie, J. (2009). *Visible learning: A synthesis of over 800 meta-analyses relating to achievement.* New York, NY: Routledge.

Hattie, J. (2012). *Visible learning for teachers.* New York, NY: Routledge.

Hattie, J. (2013). Why are so many of our teachers and schools so successful? *John Hattie at TEDxNorrkoping.* Retrieved from https://www.youtube.com/watch?v=rzwJXUieD0U&t=422s

Hattie, J., & Timperley, H. (2007). The power of feedback. *Review of Educational Research, 77*(1), 81–112.

Huang, Z. (1991). *A meta-analysis of self-questioning strategies* (Unpublished doctoral dissertation). Hofstra University, Hempstead, NY.

Hunter, M. (1967). *Teach more—faster!* Thousand Oaks, CA: Corwin Press.

Hunter, M. (1982). *Mastery teaching.* El Segundo, CA: TIP Publications.

Johnson, D. W., & Johnson, R. T. (2009). An educational psychology success story: Social interdependence theory and cooperative learning. *Journal of Educational Researcher, 38*(5), 365–379.

Kluger, A. N., & DeNisi, A. (1996). The effects of feedback interventions on performance: A historical review, meta-analysis, and a preliminary feedback intervention theory. *Psychological Bulletin, 119*(2), 254.

Knowles, M. S. (1984). *The modern practice of adult education: From pedagogy to andragogy.* Wilton, CT: Association Press.

Kulhavy, R. W. (1997). Feedback in written instruction. *Review of Educational Research, 47*(2), 211–232.

Kumar, D. D. (1991). A meta-analysis of the relationship between science instruction and student engagement. *Educational Review, 43*(1), 49–61.

Lane, H. B., & Allen, S. (2010). The vocabulary-rich classroom: Modeling sophisticated word use to promote word consciousness and vocabulary growth. *The Reading Teacher, 63*(5), 362–370.

Larson, M. R., & Kanold, T. D. (2016). *Balancing the equation: A guide to school mathematics for educators and parents.* Bloomington, IN: Solution Tree.

Leithwood, K., Seashore Louis, K., Anderson, S., & Wahlstrom, K. (2004) Review of research: How leadership influences student learning. *Learning from Leadership project.* Commissioned by The Wallace Foundation. Retrieved from: https://www.wallacefoundation.org/knowledge-center/Documents/How-Leadership-Influences-Student-Learning.pdf

Lencioni, P. (2012). *The advantage: Why organizational health trumps everything else in business.* San Francisco, CA: Jossey-Bass.

Locke, E. A., & Latham, G. P. (1990). *A theory of goal setting and task performance.* Englewood Cliffs, NJ: Prentice Hall.

Marzano, R. J. (1998). *A theory-based meta-analysis of research on instruction.* Aurora, CO: Mid-Continent Regional Education Lab.

Marzano, R. J. (2000). *A new era of school reform: Going where the research takes us.* Aurora, CO: Mid-Continent Regional Education Lab.

McTighe, J., & Wiggins, G. (2012). *Understanding by Design framework* [White paper]. Retrieved from ASCD: https://www.ascd.org/ASCD/pdf/siteASCD/publications/UbD_WhitePaper0312.pdf

Morrison, J. (2008/2009). Why teachers must be data experts. *Educational Leadership, 66*(4).

Nagy, W. E. (1988). *Teaching vocabulary to improve reading comprehension.* Urbana, IL: NCTE.

National Association for the Education of Young Children. (2009). *Developmentally appropriate practice in early childhood programs serving children from birth through age 8.* Washington, DC: Author.

National Center on Scaling Up Effective Schools (NCSU). (2014). Developing student ownership and responsibility in high schools (Practitioner brief). Nashville, TN: NCSU.

National Council of Teachers of Mathematics. (2000). *Principles and standards for school mathematics.* Reston, VA: Author.

National Governors Association Center for Best Practices & Council of Chief State School Officers. (2010a). *Common Core State Standards for English language arts and literacy in history/social studies, science, and technical subjects.* Washington, DC: Authors.

National Governors Association Center for Best Practices & Council of Chief State School Officers. (2010b). *Common Core State Standards for English language arts and literacy in history/social studies, science, and technical subjects: Appendix A.* Washington, DC: Authors.

National Governors Association Center for Best Practices & Council of Chief State School Officers. (2010c). *Common Core State Standards for mathematics.* Washington, DC: Authors.

National Governors Association Center for Best Practices & Council of Chief State School Officers. (2013). *K–8 publishers' criteria for the Common Core State Standards for mathematics.* Washington, DC: Authors.

National Mathematics Advisory Panel. (2008). *Foundations for success: The final report of the National Mathematics Advisory Panel.* Washington, DC: Department of Education.

National Research Council. (2001). *Adding it up: Helping children learn mathematics.* Washington, DC: National Academies Press. https://doi.org/10.17226/9822.

Newell, A. (1990). *Unified theories of cognition.* Cambridge, MA: Harvard University Press.

Niemi, D., Vallone, J., Wang, J., & Griffin, N. (2007). Recommendations for building a valid benchmark assessment system: Interim report to the Jackson public schools. *CRESST Report 723.* National Center for Research on Evaluation, Standards, and Student Testing (CRESST). University of California, Los Angeles.

Nuthall, G. (2005). The cultural myths and realities of classroom teaching and learning: A personal journey. *Teachers College Record, 107*(5), 895–934.

Nuthall, G. (2007). *The hidden lives of learners.* Wellington, New Zealand: NZCER Press.

O'Connell, M., & Vandos, K. (2015). *Partnering with students: Building ownership of learning.* Thousand Oaks, CA: Corwin Press.

Office of Superintendent of Public Instruction–Washington State. (2010). *Standards for mathematical practices progression through grade levels.* Retrieved from https://www.masonk12.net/sites/default/files/documents/Buildings/CO/wa%20smp%20unpacked%20k-12.pdf

Parsons, J., & Taylor, L. (2011). Improving student engagement. *Current Issues in Education, 14*(1). Retrieved from https://cie.asu.edu/ojs/index.php/cieatasu/issue/view/12

Purkey, W. W., & Stanley, P. H. (1991). *Invitational teaching, learning, and living.* Washington, DC: NEA.

RAND Education. (2012). *Teachers matter: Understanding teachers' impact on student achievement.* Santa Monica, CA: RAND. Retrieved from https://www.rand.org/pubs/corporate_pubs/CP693z1-2012-09.html

Reeves, D. (2018). *Engaging every learner* (presentation). San Bernardino City Unified School District. Retrieved from University of California, San Bernardino and www.CreativeLeadership.net

Risko, V. J., & Vogt, M. (2016). *Professional learning in action: An inquiry approach for teachers of literacy.* New York, NY: Teachers College Press.

Robinson, V. (2011). *Student-centered leadership.* San Francisco, CA: Jossey-Bass.

Rosenshine, B., & Meister, C. (1994). Reciprocal teaching: A review of the research. *Review of Educational Research, 64*(4), 479–530.

Rothman, R. (2011). *Something in common: The Common Core standards and the next chapter in American education.* Cambridge, MA: Harvard Education Press.

Samson, G. E., Strykowski, B., Weinstein, T., & Walberg, H. J. (1987). The effects of teacher questioning levels on student achievement: A quantitative synthesis. *Journal of Educational Research, 80*(5), 290–295.

Schemel, R. (1997). *Management training exercise: From theory to practice.* Ankara, Turkey: Turkish Psychological Association.

Schmoker, M. J. (2016). *Leading with focus: Elevating the essentials for school and district improvement.* Alexandria, VA: ASCD.

Schön, D. A. (1983). *The reflective practitioner: How professionals think in action.* New York, NY: Basic Books.

Scott, J. A., Skobel, B. J., & Wells, J. (2008). *The word-conscious classroom: Building the vocabulary readers and writers need.* New York, NY: Scholastic.

Seidel, T., & Shavelson, R. J. (2007). Teaching effectiveness research in the past decade: The role of theory and research and research design in disentangling meta-analysis results. *Review of Educational Research, 77*(4), 454–499.

Shanahan, T. (2012). *Shanahan on literacy* (Web log). Retrieved from http://www.shanahanonliteracy.com/2012/06/what-is-close-reading.html

Stevens, R. J., & Slavin, R. E. (1990). When cooperative learning improves the achievement of students with mild disabilities: A response to Tateyama-Sniezek. *Exceptional Children, 57*(3), 276–280.

Stronge, J. H. (Ed.). (2006). Teacher evaluation and school improvement: Improving the educational landscape. In *Evaluating teaching: A guide to current thinking and best practice* (pp. 1–23, 2nd ed.). Thousand Oaks, CA: Corwin Press.

Stronge, J. H., & Helm, V. M. (1992). A performance evaluation system for professional support personnel. *Educational Evaluation and Policy Analysis, 14,* 175–180.

Swanson, H. L., & Hoskyn, M. (1998). Experimental intervention research on students with learning disabilities: A meta-analysis of treatment outcomes. *Review of Educational Research, 68*(3), 277–321.

Test, J. E., Cunningham, D. D., & Lee, A. C. (2010). Talking with young children: How teachers encourage learning. *Dimensions of Early Childhood, 38*(3), 3–14.

Thomas, R. S. (2011). My nine 'truths' of data analysis: Data-driven strategies alone won't boost student achievement. *Education Week Spotlight, 30*(35), 29, 36.

Timperley, H. (2011). *Realizing the power of professional learning.* New York, NY: Open University Press.

Tomlinson, C. A. (2017). *How to differentiate instruction in academically diverse classrooms.* Alexandria, VA: ASCD.

Vega, V. (2015). *Teacher development research review: Keys to educator success.* Edutopia: George Lucas Educational Foundation. Retrieved from https://www.edutopia.org /teacher-development-research-keys-success

Vescio, V., Ross, D., & Adams, A. (2008). A review of research on the impact of professional learning communities on teaching practice and student learning. *Teaching and Teacher Education, 24*(2008), 80–91.

Walker, D., Greenwood, C., Hart, B., & Carta, J. (1994). Prediction of school outcomes based on early language production and socioeconomic factors. *Child Development, 65*(2), 606–621.

Wallace Foundation. (2013). *The school principal as leader: Guiding schools to better teaching and learning.* Retrieved from: https://www.wallacefoundation.org /knowledge-center/pages/the-school-principal-as-leader-guiding-schools-to -better-teaching-and-learning.aspx

Weimer, M. (2012). *Deep learning vs. surface learning: Getting students to understand the difference.* Retrieved from the Teaching Professor Blog: http://www.facultyfocus .com/articles/teaching-professor-blog/deep-learning-vs-surface-learning-getting -students-to-understand-the-difference/

Whitmore, J. (2017). *Coaching for performance: The principles and practice of coaching and leadership.* Boston, MA: Nicholas Brealey Publishing.

Wiggins, G., & McTighe, J. (2005). *Understanding by design.* Alexandria, VA: ASCD.

Zwiers, J., & Crawford, M. (2011). *Academic conversations: Classroom talk that fosters critical thinking and content understandings.* Portland, ME: Stenhouse.

APPENDIX

List of Figures and Tables

All tables listed in bold can be downloaded and used as tools when planning, implementing, and reflecting on the actions of instructional leadership. They can be downloaded at www.elevatedachievement.com.